Grace
Peace
Balance

Surviving and *Thriving* Against All Odds

Grace
Peace
Balance

Surviving and *Thriving* Against All Odds

GABY ABDELGADIR

TAG Publishing, LLC
2030 S. Milam
Amarillo, TX 79109
www.TAGPublishers.com

Office (806) 373-0114
Fax (806) 373-4004
info@TAGPublishers.com

ISBN: 978-1-59930-429-8

Text: Lloyd Arbour, www.mynewart.com

First Edition

Contents

Dedication

I dedicate this book to my one and only son Michael who brings joy to my heart and who I believe is my biggest gift from God. Mikey, I love you so much!

Foreword

Gaby Abdelgadir understands the true meaning of finding inner peace. That doesn't mean her journey has been easy, nor does it mean that she takes life for granted.

Often, we allow the urgent business of life to get in the way of what is really important and as Gaby knows, life can quickly bring us back into understanding through difficult circumstances.

I've been a serious student of the mind and have spent virtually all of my adult life studying human behavior: why we do the things we do and don't do some of the things we know will bring us better results. We have deep reservoirs of potential lying dormant within and all we need is the key to unlock it. *Grace, Peace, and Balance: Surviving and Thriving Against All Odds* is the story of one woman's journey in her quest for balance.

We all want to explore our dreams and live an abundant life but so many are too afraid to do so. Gaby had every excuse to fail. She came from a war-torn part of the world and had experienced more by the time she was a teen than most people experience their whole lives. Still, she was undeterred and set out to make a new life in a country half-way around the world. She is a striking example of what's possible when you make an irrevocable decision to step out of your comfort zone and go for your dreams. Through the heartache and struggles, Gaby clung to the knowledge that she had a glorious purpose that as yet had been defined.

When we release our fear and choose to live on purpose, rather than by default, we put ourselves in a position to unleash our true potential and create the life we choose. To meet Gaby today and see the joy for life that radiates from her being, you would never guess the trauma she has endured. She is a testament to the strength that we all possess to be a beacon of light in the world.

Grace, Peace, and Balance: Surviving and Thriving Against All Odds shows us how to overcome and thrive no matter the circumstances or obstacles that life introduces along the way. Gaby shows each of us how to cling to that which endures in our lives instead of those things we think are important at the time. All of the things we may accumulate in our lifetime . . . money, cars, houses and stuff . . . serve a purpose in our lives and reward us for our hard work and achievement. And though these things make our lives more comfortable and we enjoy them, our family, friends, and love are what sustain us through life. This book will help you understand the power and strength each of us has to recreate our lives into something beautiful.

– Bob Proctor, Featured Teacher in
The Secret* and Best Selling Author of *You Were Born Rich

Chapter 1

Chapter 1

Life's Challenges

In life, there will always be challenges. As much as life can be full of wonderful and happy surprises, it can also be equally full of the total opposite.

Khartoum, Sudan was home for me until I finished first grade. My memories of those years were very happy. My dad owned several jewelry stores so he spent a great deal of time working late in the evenings. Most nights, he wouldn't get home until about 8:00 pm. My brother and I always went to bed at around 7:30 pm, so I pretended to be asleep until I heard him come home. As soon as the door opened, I ran out of my bedroom to hug my dad. I also asked for a dollar. As soon as I got my dollar, I would ask him to give me a dollar for my brother (who was already asleep by then). I took my brother's money and placed it under his pillow.

Those good times were short lived, however, and even as a young girl I was soon to learn about life's challenges. My mother was Ethiopian, absolutely beautiful, amazingly elegant, always serious, very organized, one of the neatest people that I have ever known and completely fearless and dominating. My father, on the other hand, was of Turkish origin with his grandmother being of Moroccan background. He was tall and handsome with hazel brown eyes and my parents were a very striking couple. My father was wealthy and one of the most generous people that I could have known. But like so many people, while he had some wonderfully redeeming qualities, he also had his share of weaknesses. In my father's case, his weakness was beautiful women.

At about six years old, I vaguely remember many people visiting us at home on a daily basis and having long conversations with my mom. With each visit, my mother became increasingly upset. I watched close friends kneel down beside her and plead with her. I had no idea what they were asking her. I just remember her saying "No, I have made my mind up and nothing is going to change it!"

It wasn't until my mother told us later that we were moving, I realized what was going on. She finally had enough of my father's jealousy and infidelity and did not want us to witness the kind of dysfunctional life she and my father shared. We flew to Asmara, the capital city of Eritrea where my mother arranged to change our family name (my brother and I) because she wanted to make sure that my father couldn't petition for custody. Little did my mom know how damaging this name change was going to be for our future - especially for my brother.

We moved to Asmara in the summer, so mother hired a private teacher to come to our rented home every day. This teacher taught us the Ethiopian alphabets and how to read and write the language. At the end of summer, my brother and I were tested and registered in one of the best Catholic Schools in the country. I was accepted in the girls' school for Grade 2. My brother joined the boys' school and surprised the administrators with how well he tested. Instead of Grade 6, they put him in Grade 7. The only time he moved to a lower class was for the Amharic language class where his language was a Grade 3 level.

I was always the happy and cheerful one of the family so these changes didn't affect me as much because I loved people and made friends easily. My brother, on the other hand, was my total opposite. He was always a loner and didn't like anybody touching him, let alone hugging or kissing him so he took these changes much harder than I did. Even now, it is surprising to me how two people born from the same mother could be so different.

I have heard it said repeatedly that multi-cultured children turn out to be very smart. I am not sure if it is the exposure to numerous languages and cultures at an early age or not, but there does seem to be some correlation and my brother exemplified that. He was always an A+ student even having only learned the local language a few months earlier. In fact, he eventually became fluent in seven languages. He learned very quickly and skipped the 6th grade, 8th grade and 10th grade.

I believed that one of the reasons he did so well was that I always viewed him as my mother's favorite. They were very much alike, personality wise, as my mother had trouble showing affection and was supremely intelligent and my brother exhibited this same personality. He is a little over five years older than me and while I was always an A student I didn't understand or speak seven languages and I had to apply myself, where it seemed to be completely natural for him. He could read a 600 page book in a few hours while it took me a few days to a week, making me slow and stupid – something that he mentioned frequently as older siblings will often do to younger ones.

During this time, I missed my father so very much. I cried almost every day and called for him. This was especially true every time my mother and brother teased me or upset me. My father had always been someone I could run to and feel safe with being suddenly without him, I felt very alone. It took me at least three years to come to terms with the fact that I would never see him again. It is a hard thing for a child to accept and the result often manifests itself much like the stages of grief for truly, it was as if he had died.

What I didn't know until I was in my late teens was that my mother hid the fact that my dad frequently visited Asmara and I could have easily met him. She believed any contact I had with him would be detrimental but I look back on it now and see that my mother's fear ruled some of the decisions she made. I don't blame her for being hurt and wanting to be out of a relationship such as they had but, as is often the case, parents inflict pain on children no matter the decision they make at the time and she didn't realize how much it hurt me in particular. Being without a father was in many ways much worse to me than if he had died. That is because I knew he was still out there, and still loved me, but I just couldn't be with him or see him.

This sense of abandonment, though at the time was difficult, I thought I would overcome and moved on with my life. I didn't realize that once I was also a parent and was faced with unimaginable crisis, that these same fears would reenter my thoughts and life, with a vengeance.

In the spring of 2005, I was living in Canada having fully immigrated in 1997 and became a Canadian citizen. Canada seemed to be the land of opportunity coming from such a war torn and unstable region of the world as I had. Not long after I was in Canada I met my husband Mulugeta (called Muler by friends and family). Shortly thereafter we were blessed with a wonderful child and though our life wasn't perfect, it offered the promise of a good life.

Gaby Abdelgadir

Early in 2005, my husband started complaining about stomach pains. He thought the pain was caused by the type of food he was eating, so he wasn't too alarmed. But this didn't make sense to me. I hadn't changed the way I cooked, or ingredients I was using since we first met. He didn't have any pain before, so why would he suddenly have pain? My initial thought was that he developed heart burn as he aged and as a result of being stressed at work all the time, so I bought him different types of over the counter anti-acid medications from the drug store. He agreed to try the medicine and it worked for about an hour each time but then the pain would return. This went on for weeks and I began to have a disturbing feeling it was much more. After so many days of him being in excruciating pain, I asked him to go to his doctor to find out the cause of his pain.

Muler never liked to visit doctors unless it was considered an extreme emergency and I can't say I blame him for that as no one wants to be poked and prodded, but this seemed serious to me. While he put it off, I continuously asked him to make an appointment with his doctor – you might say I nagged him and that would be true. But I just knew this wasn't right. After two months of constant reminders and nagging from me, he finally made an appointment. His doctor however, didn't even bother to undertake any tests or send him to a specialist. Instead, she just prescribed him a one month supply of medicine to supposedly help stop the pain. I was irritated and annoyed more than anything as she had no idea how hard it was for me to get him to go see her in the first place! Didn't she think we had tried medicine and seen that there was something else going on? Still, if by some miracle this medicine worked then that was fine, so he started the medication.

Muler took his medication daily for a month but there was no change and he continued to complain of stomach pains. Nothing had changed and to me, it seemed worse. I encouraged him to go back to the doctor and insist on tests, but he was reluctant. If the first time hadn't worked, why go again, he argued. It took another month of me pleading with him to make another appointment with his doctor before he finally did return. I think by this time he knew it was more than heartburn just as I did and that it wasn't getting better. When he came home from the doctor this time, I was in for another shock. His doctor prescribed *another* one month supply of the *same* medication!

When I asked him why he came back with the same medicine that he already tried which didn't work, his reply was, "My doctor was surprised it didn't work for me as it works for most people and insisted I have to take it again! She is the doctor not you!"

It was obvious he was angry and deep down I think he was hoping that I really was wrong and that this medicine just needed more time to work. I held my silence this time as I knew he had to go through with her instructions. He repeated the medication for another month but with no success and in fact, his pains grew increasingly worse.

It is extremely hard to watch a loved one suffer and know that you can't do anything to help. We were both working and had a young son to tend to and the stress of my husband being constantly ill wore on all of us. But this experience taught me many valuable lessons, the most important of which was to trust myself and my own instincts. I knew we were wasting time as he tried to self-diagnose his pain. I felt it. Time was ticking by and I had a panic in my chest having to stand by and watch.

Muler didn't want to contradict the doctor, but I learned very quickly that no one will care more about your health or your life than you and I knew that Muler needed help. I wanted to scream and yell and insist that more be done. I knew something was wrong and deep down I think so did he but it's hard to confront a supposed 'professional' especially when your health is concerned. I honestly think that Muler hoped it would just go away or be some sort of an easy fix. Part of it was denial and part of it was fear. I was afraid too, but I also knew that putting off finding the real problem might even make it worse. I told him that I would be happy to go and do the talking on his behalf so we could get to the bottom of the issue. While he declined my offer, I think he finally accepted and understood that I was right and this wasn't going away. He went back to the doctor, and this time he was referred to a specialist for an endoscopy.

Within a few days, Muler had the test done and then we waited. I wondered what they might say, if he had an ulcer or some type of chronic acid problem. Finally, four days after he had had the endoscopy, we received an urgent call from the specialist for him to go back immediately. I was afraid, but Muler said it was silly of me to worry too much and that I should just go on to work, rejecting my offer to go with him. I did go to work but I didn't hear back from him during the day and I was getting more and more concerned every minute.

After work, I picked up our five year old son, Michael, from daycare and we arrived home. When we walked in, Muler was busy on the phone talking to one of his closest friends. I went straight to him and asked "So?" and he whispered "later" but I was insistent and said "No, now!" I had been worried sick the entire day and now he wanted me to wait for him to finish his conversation on the phone? *I mean, seriously?* When he saw how serious I was, he put his friend on hold and whispered in a calm and casual tone, "I have both an ulcer and cancer".

I thought he was joking and didn't appreciate it after worrying the whole day. Frustrated, I angrily said to him, "This is not funny!"

He looked at me and I remember how the sadness suddenly showed on his face. He then calmly told me he wasn't joking.

I was completely and utterly stunned. I don't really remember what happened the next few hours and days as I just walked around in a kind of stupor trying to wrap my mind around the diagnosis. I was walking around like a zombie and was very quiet. I didn't feel like I could go on and had no idea what was next. I made all sorts of assumptions that my life was never meant to be a good and a happy one as all these challenges and obstacles kept on jumping in my path. I was exhausted from thinking too much and from the fear that was creeping into my heart. My road seemed filled with disappointments, discouragements and fear.

It wasn't long though before I realized that I had to pull myself together. My husband was sick and needed me. My young son needed me. I didn't have the luxury to withdraw and lick my wounds - I had to find a way through the obstacles that life put in front of me. I resolved to get up each day, focus on that day and get through it, then start again the next day. And it worked. Slowly but surely, I found myself walking through the motions of keeping our lives and our family moving forward and although the path was wretchedly hard at times, that determination would serve me well.

The Paralysis of Fear

I quickly learned that sitting and worrying about my problems didn't solve anything. In fact, it grew a small kernel of fear into a huge mountain. I had to take action, even if that action was just to get myself out of bed each day and stop wallowing in sadness. I realized the failure to take action keeps us stagnate and unable to see the next step. I realized that some people are simply scared to take action and have constant doubts swirling in their heads.

I know this because it is exactly the way I used to be. I feared almost everything and everyone and I will admit that there are times that fear still creeps back in. The fear of moving forward can cripple us and it threatened to do just that to me after Muler's diagnosis. Most of us would rather stay in our comfort zone than to step out into the unknown and I get that, but there are times the unknown is the only path and you must travel it whether you want to or not.

If you are paralyzed by fear then consider this "how much pain is associated with not taking action?" Most people focus on the pain of taking action rather than the freedom that comes because of it. I knew I had no control over Muler's disease, yet I sat and wallowed in my own sadness for some time. I had to find faith and hope and apply those beliefs to deliberate action. When times are bleak, we tend to forget that our attitude is the sum of our feelings and our actions, and it starts with a *thought*. When adversity enters our lives, often times we react rather than respond. Think about a time when you reacted in haste and regretted it. How different would that situation have been if you could have taken a moment and responded with deliberate action?

To prevail, we have to grow larger than our current place and circumstances and live from the inside – on purpose, rather than in a reactive state just defending ourselves from what life throws our way. Every day offers new opportunities for us to find our "why" for persisting and succeeding through life's challenges and until you know that 'why' you can find yourself repeating the same patterns over and over. My 'why' was my son Michael. No matter what happened to my husband or myself, my son deserved better. He deserved parents that were present and aware in his life – not some shell shocked zombies hoping for the best!

With our focus dedicated to overcoming life's challenges, we are set to prevail in any circumstance. We must appreciate both the highs and the lows because they both are equally important. The rain must fall in order for life to flourish. Some people however, focus only on the rain, not realizing that the sunshine lurks behind the clouds. The blackest night will always turn into day. Yet it is the dark of night that gives us rest and restores our energy for the coming daylight. There is a time for tears and a time for joy. The night never lasts and neither does our times of sorrow. We don't question the seasons or the changing of day into night, but we so often question and doubt those times in our lives when we must go through periods of sorrow. I am guilty myself as on more than one occasion I have said *"Why me?"* I wanted a reason for all of my pain and suffering; for all the challenges that I keep facing. I didn't want to accept the fact that hurt and anguish were part of life's natural cycle.

What was the old saying that I heard growing up? *"When it rains it pours"?*

This seemed to be very true in my life as one challenge seemed to be quickly followed by another and another. Yes, more bad news kept on flowing. I remember reading a quote that said, "What you resist, persists."

Let me tell you that the hard times were certainly persistent. It got to the point that instead of hoping for good news, we were *resisting* hearing more bad news. Have you done this? Instead of imagining a great outcome, you just hoped it didn't go completely downhill? This is what the quote means. By resisting more bad news instead of focusing on expecting good news, we bring that bad into being with our thoughts and attitudes. At the time, I didn't understand it this way. But now I do – and I do very well!

The great paradox is that we can't appreciate the light without the dark. It is funny that often we grow the most during very hard circumstance and I learned a good deal about myself during the days of Muler's illness. When we go through a period of trial, rest assured that it is nothing more than a season and with patience, the time will pass and we will be prepared for the new experiences that lie ahead of us. Remember, weeping may last through the night, but joy comes with the morning. Expect the joy to follow as surely as night turns into day.

Gaby Abdelgadir

Enduring Strength

It is true that we are the only ones in charge of our happiness and if we want to prevail, we must learn to create our best life - regardless of the circumstances surrounding it. Peace comes from the inside not the other way around. To create a happy and balanced life, we have to find that happiness internally and stop letting external factors dictate our emotional state. We can't allow our bank accounts, living arrangements, relationships, careers or (especially in my situation) a catastrophic illness, followed by a major financial struggle, take away our faith and strength. To live internally, we first have to change our thought process and overtime this change in perception will allow us to create the life we want. By focusing on this goal we become proactive in our own lives instead of reactive to external forces.

Unfortunately, most of us have been groomed to live according to external circumstances. We are taught by our parents, teachers, siblings and even neighbors to consider *everyone else* before attending to *our own needs* and desires, and we often find ourselves, at some point or another, questioning what it is that we need to make our own lives fulfilled. I think everyone, even in good circumstances; on occasion realizes that life didn't turn out exactly like they thought it would. We all have the possibility to live from the inside; it is just a matter of whether we are ready to do so and honestly many of us aren't ready for a number of years.

We have to learn and grow – and yes, experience some of the hard aspects of life – before we are really ready to take control and change things. However, if we choose to prevail under any circumstance then the world is wide open to our dreams. Living from the inside requires effort to look beyond any dark season that may come our way and be able to find peace sometimes in the midst of extreme chaos.

Remember that after every storm, shines a rainbow - full of beautiful colors.

Once we learn to live from the inside, our lives dramatically improve. I am filled with so much energy and inspiration, and it is a true privilege to be able to use my darkest hours to help others find their own sun. It is my sincere wish for everyone I meet to be filled with the same inspiration, passion and purpose. Each of our journeys will be different, but as long as we reach the same destination, our lives will be lived to the fullest.

Through faith, God tells us to stand firm in any circumstance because we have a purpose. God wants all of His children to fulfill their destiny which is why He gave us the ability to program our minds to persist. As I learned through my husband's cancer, we are conquerors - so how can we allow ourselves to quit with that knowledge?

Persistence is one of the most important character traits we can possess and the great news is that we each can develop the mental attitude necessary to persist. Prevailing and succeeding through adversity requires us to maintain a strong focus on our goals and take daily steps toward those goals. There are countless books about persistence and as I wrote this section, I wondered, "How can I make my take on persistence different than what has been said a million times?" As I pondered what to write, the question "*why*" kept coming to me. I took that as a sign and decided to focus on the "why" rather than the "how".

So the question is, *Why persist*? What is our biggest reason to keep on going?

LESSON # 1:

When life seems to throw on us the unwanted and the unexpected, we have to be strong. We have to have faith in ourselves that we can overcome and face any challenges that we come across. Most of all, we have to have faith in God. We have to know and believe that we are never alone and that God will always be there for us. He will give us the strength and will pave a way for us to handle any challenges we may come across.

Chapter 2

Chapter 2

Having Faith

Often times, we don't accomplish our dreams and goals because we are conditioned to believe we are limited in one way or another. Low self esteem and lack of self worth are just a few of the myriad ways we limit ourselves. Once we let these thoughts enter our minds, and for many of us they were programmed at a very young age, they take over our thought process and crowd out any positive feelings. Lack-based thoughts including fear, guilt, and insecurities, can take over our lives and rob us of happiness. I know for me, I have allowed sabotaging thoughts to steal my dreams on more than one occasion.

The key to living a life of fulfillment is to eliminate our destructive thoughts. For too many people, the mere idea of changing their thought process may sound impossible. Once I learned about the power of thought, insecurities would often take over and fear kept me from truly believing that it was possible to change my own thought process.

I would wonder, How *can I change the thoughts I have carried with me my entire life?* I wondered that even if I could change, why should I work so hard to control my negative thoughts and desires, my life isn't *all* that bad. The answer was simple, those negative thoughts and desires transform into words and words result in action and so by allowing those negative thoughts to remain I was bringing more negative into my life.

> *Be positive or be quiet. You can't talk defeat and expect something positive. If you don't have anything good to say about yourself or your life, zip it up and be quiet. Don't verbalize it.*
>
> **- Pastor Joel Osteen**

When someone has a lot of negative thoughts, it leads to stress, anxiety, depression, negative actions and an overall sense that something is missing in their life.

Understanding that the ability to choose our thoughts is the primary skill we can learn to *replace* our destructive thoughts with positive and encouraging ones that enable us to create the life we desire.

Without this skill, we succumb to all of the "I can'ts or I don'ts" rattling around in our minds. Our self-imposed limitations often stem from society or events in our early childhood that are still affecting us.

For instance, when I was a little girl, my mother and brother led me to believe that I was adopted. At the time they were playing and teasing, but to me they seemed so serious that I started to believe it. They both told me this story repeatedly; that I was found crying next to a garage bin (I mean seriously? No better place to find me than next to a garbage bin?). The story continued on that they just couldn't leave such a cute baby there, so they decided to take me home to raise me as their own. To them, it was a sweet story of how irresistibly cute I was and showed that they chose to have me in the family, but that is not what I heard. I heard I was abandoned and unwanted and they were stuck with me.

They thought it was all in good natured fun but it *wasn't* because I really believed the story and started to build resentment toward both of them. My nanny at the time, told me that it was not true and that they were just making up the story to upset and tease me. She swore repeatedly that my mom was actually my biological mother. But who did I believe? Like any young child, I believed my mother and brother. With this destructive thought process in place, my mind conjured up falsities about our relationship. For example, I always felt left out when both my mother and brother would play cards or have long conversations. Jealousy crowded my thoughts and I convinced myself that I didn't belong with them. Of course, as an adult, I can look back and see that my mother and brother simply had a lot in common and got on extremely well. They didn't intentionally leave me out, but my personality was quite different than theirs and to me that meant I was an outsider. I was also almost six years younger than my brother and that age difference meant that we often couldn't be involved in the same activities which just added to my sense of loneliness.

We lived in a relatively conservative part of the world where a girl's reputation is very important. I remember my brother once convinced my mother to take me out of piano classes because I was too wild and he thought the music classes may cause me to run off with a crazy band during my teenage years. Those days, anything my brother said to my mother was considered to be the gospel and as a result, she took me out of piano lessons. I cried for weeks, every night before I went to bed and whenever I got a chance to be alone. I thought to myself that this confirms that I am adopted because if I was her "real" daughter, she wouldn't have listened to my brother and I would still be going for my piano lessons. To be an accomplished pianist is yet a dream I am determined to fulfill – even if it means I will be in my eighties!

It is interesting that when we believe something to be true, our minds will look at the circumstances of any event and fit them to that belief. Of course my family loved me, but they weren't perfect. They were just people with their faults and short comings as any family would have. But my mind was convinced that they didn't love me so everything I heard or saw fed that belief.

In addition to the adoption story, my mother also told me that I was a mistake and that she never wanted a second child – let alone a girl. I also overheard her talk with her friends about this particular subject repeatedly. This added to my resentment for a very long time and yet, I always looked up to my mother and always sought her approval. I can look back and see the concern she had raising not only a son, but a daughter on her own in a location and culture that was difficult and unstable at times. I know now she was voicing her frustration with a marriage that didn't work out and with the fact that raising children as a single mother was extremely challenging.

Still, as a child, I remember always repeating to myself silently "wait until I grow up – I won't need both of you!" I lived with this skewed view of the love my family had for me and so I had a very negative perspective of my own worth. Far too many people's minds are skewed in just this same way because somebody's outside opinion altered their perception of their self worth. But what if that person decided to "break the rules" one day and change those thoughts? What if they accept, as I did, that those negative thoughts are their own perception of the situation and often have nothing to do with reality? More than likely their life would improve rather than disintegrate into ashes.

Failure to understand the mind creates fear in so many people and what it really boils down to is the fear of the unknown.

Later on in life when I was an adult, I *confronted* my mother with how I had felt as a child. She was sad and very shocked that I kept these thoughts and emotions in my heart for all those years. She sat me down and told me that growing up, I was a real tomboy and that she was seriously worried I may end up running away with some crazy band group or something similar like my brother told her. She wanted to keep me safe and be a good mother. She also told me that they were only teasing me about the adoption and never thought for a second that I would take it that seriously and hold on to it for all those years. It was at that point I realized my own responsibility in my perceptions.

I have to admit that I was really considered a tomboy so I can see her concern was valid. I always enjoyed playing with boys in sports such as soccer, basketball, racing and so forth and this was considered a big "NO NO" in my upbringing. I was a girl and I was supposed to act like a lady! Her actions showed her deep concern for my well being but I interpreted each one as some sort of negative proof that I wasn't good enough when nothing could have been further from the truth.

Create Your Own Destiny

Sometimes we look at others and think that we would like to have our lives be just like theirs, but at the same time think that it's just not possible. We think that other people were born better off, or had more advantages, or were just plain lucky. What many of us don't realize though is that we have the power to create any type of life we want. The thoughts we currently hold in our minds are what has brought about the results in our lives and so if we aren't happy, we only have our own thoughts to blame.

The good news is that once we realize that we can create our own happiness, then the fear of the expectation of others tends to go away. We no longer worry what someone else might think, we just go for it! To change our results, we first have to change what is flowing into our minds. It may seem like a single thought is really insignificant, but in truth we have tens of thousands of thoughts each day so they really add up.

However, when faced with crisis, sometimes it can seem like you are running uphill with no end in sight.

By the end of January of 2008, Muler was in Palliative Care at Princess Margaret Hospital, Toronto. He had fought hard over the last few years, but the cancer had won. It was only a matter of time now. One morning, he begged me to get permission from the hospital to come home for an overnight. He had missed being home with his family and friends so badly, so I spoke with his doctor and the nurses and they agreed to let me take him home for one night and then bring him back the next morning. With a handful of medications and specific instructions for his care in hand, we left for home.

I was very happy to make Muler's wish come true although it was nothing compared to his happiness to go home one more time. It really seemed like a dream – as if maybe things would be like they were before, even if deep down we know they would not.

Once we got home, Muler was craving a certain type of a meal (different from what he ate at the hospital) and I made it for him. He ate with excitement. The portion he ate was really small but it made him very happy. We smiled and just enjoyed each other's company. About an hour after eating his meal, he became extremely ill. I was shocked and scared. When he underwent chemo he often had a hard time holding things down, but he wasn't on chemo and now his sickness seemed uncontrollable. I immediately felt guilty for cooking him a meal that maybe he shouldn't have eaten. I just wanted him to be happy, even if only for a moment. But was that selfish on my part? I convinced myself that his sudden illness was all my fault.

Soon, Muler was choking up blood and panic really set in for me. Crying, I rushed to call the hospital but he begged me not to contact his doctor or the nurses. He didn't want to go back to the hospital. He wanted to sleep at home for just that one night. How could I deny him a last wish? So I put the phone down. His sickness subsided after a while and I helped him wash up. He finally went to bed to rest a little bit. A few minutes later, it started again. More blood. I helped him to bed again. When I went to the room to see him a few minutes later, his mouth was open and blood was flowing out of his mouth, soaking the pillow, bed spread and down to the carpet on the floor! At this point I ignored his pleas to not get help and was on the phone with the Palliative Care unit explaining to them, all while choking back my own tears, what was happening. They told me it was expected as the cancer had spread everywhere and that it had nothing to do with what he ate at this point. They then instructed me to take him back to the hospital immediately.

As soon as I hang up the phone, there was a knock on the door. It was a family member and a friend. When they had gone to the hospital to visit Muler and were told he was home for one night, they came all the way to our home. I invited them in but told them that I really couldn't entertain them as I normally would. I could see they were worried and a bit scared after observing my nervousness and terrified expression.

Over every mountain there is a path,
although it may not be seen from the valley.

– **Theodore Roethke**
Teacher, Poet, Author, 1908 – 1963

To this day I believe that their visit was a miracle from God. He had sent them to help even before I knew how desperately I would need that help. Once they were seated, I returned to the room to check on Muler and found him lying down in a different position. His eyes were completely rolled upward - to the extent that I couldn't see his pupils and that was just in the few minutes while I was on the phone! Frantically, I screamed for our friends to come help. While they were in the room with him, I ran out to call my brother-in-law, Berhane, to come over and help me take Muler back to the hospital.

Our wonderful friends meanwhile, managed to hold Muler's head, tapping him on the face slightly and talking to him, asking him to wake up. His eyes were finally back to normal but he wasn't at all aware of his surroundings. I cleaned his face, packed all the medication and we put him in a computer chair to take him downstairs. One person held his feet in the front while the other was pushing the computer chair. I packed up changes of clothing and we got into my brother-in-law's car, who was already waiting outside our parking lot. He was terrified at the scene and came running to help carry his brother to the front seat. Then we took off for the hospital.

Can you imagine if I was all alone that afternoon and if our two unexpected visitors weren't there? What would have I done? I was so happy and so very grateful! God, The Almighty, is always there for us with a solution when we need it most! *Guaranteed!*

As soon as we got to the hospital, the nurses were running around and his doctor was called in. Muler was given blood thickening medication as instructed by the doctor but it wasn't until the evening that he started to become aware of his surroundings. It took him a while to realize that he was back in the hospital and when he did, he was shocked and disappointed. The sadness in his face was unbearable for me. I wanted so badly for him to have that one last night at home and it had been a disaster. Of course, he wanted to know what happened. There were a bunch of us sitting there in his room quietly and after staring at all of us one by one, he suddenly asked why there was no music playing and why everyone was so quiet. Someone immediately jumped up and turned on some music. He didn't really want anyone to feel sorry for him and wanted music playing all the time. He enjoyed the company of his family and friends, but he also wanted them to talk – in particular about anything funny.

The doctor had instructed the nurses to call her when Muler was awake and able to communicate which they did. She arrived, sat beside him and held his hand. She was one of the kindest doctors I had seen in my life. She explained to him what they had done to stop the bleeding and what they would do the next day so that it doesn't happen again. She advised him that their plan was to do a blood transfusion as he had lost a lot of blood. His response not only shocked his family and friends sitting in the room, but it took his doctor by complete surprise. "Doctor, please don't!" he said "I do not want any more medication, treatment or anything else. The only thing I want now is pain killers. Nothing is going to change anything now anyway and I am ready to go anytime." There was silence in the room. After what it seemed forever, his doctor said, "Okay then Muler, if that is your wish, I will instruct the nurses to stop tomorrow's plan for blood transfusion. I will check on you in the morning."

That night when I got back home, I had to make sure not to let my son go to the room full of blood stains. After dinner, bath and reading time, my son finally fell asleep and I got up to clean. I removed all the bedding, put it in the washer and I got busy scrubbing every drop of blood from the mattress and the carpet. It is strange that you think when a loved one dies, you will be haunted by the day they die, but that wasn't the case for me. For the next three to four years, I had frequent nightmares of that particular day and how I scrubbed my husband's blood from everything in the bedroom. I would wake up in the middle of the night, sweating, unable to breathe. I would get out of bed, run to the kitchen for a drink of cold water and then sit down in the living room to cry and pray. I cried for Muler and for my nightmares to end. So many times, I cried so hard that my tears drenched my pillow and I frequently woke up with swollen eyes in the morning.

Peace is the result of retraining your mind to process life as it is, rather than as you think it should be.

– Dr. Wayne Dyer

There were times that I honestly thought that my mind was going to explode. It (my mind that is) was working too hard. "My mind is working too much overtime" I used to tell my friends. And this wasn't only consistent, but it went on and on for the longest period. There was a major conflict and non-stop Q&A flashing back and forth in my mind:

- Will I be able to survive all this on my own?

- *Of course you will Gaby, what on earth happened to you!*

- Am I going to be a good mother and give my son a good life all on my own?

- *Of course you will, you are going to give him more than you ever had!*

- How am I going to survive financially?

- *What happened to your Faith in God Gaby? Haven't you gone through so much in life already and yet you have survived them all? You failed and got back up again and again?*

- But I am not as healthy as I used to be – what if my health gets worse?

- *Start taking care of yourself silly! Begin by eating 3 meals a day like a normal human being and start taking some vitamins too. You also need to start some sort of an exercise – even if it is a 15 minute walk every day!*

- Oh I am so terrified of what awaits me.

- Are you the same Gaby that I know? This doesn't sound like you! What possibly could happen worse than what you have been through these past few years?

- What happens to my son if I die suddenly?

- *Can you stop thinking about all these negative things? Why can't you just relax, believe in God and pray for all the good that may be available to you?*

- I used to be one of the strongest women, very confident and always ready to face new challenges... why am I so terrified now all of a sudden?

  First off, you are still the same strong, confident, go getter, Gaby. You always had a solution for every problem that came across you. These other things are just in your head and your imagination and you need to stop them right now! Stop, stop, stop!

I know now that we are created with the gift of *choice*. We can always choose the thoughts we wish to focus on and to accept our reality. Energy flows from our mind into our bodies and emanates out into our actions and the way we act. The images we hold in our mind will most often be transmuted or materialized in physical results in our life. As you might guess, all this negative self-talk wasn't really helping me much. If anything it was scaring me to death! It is important to truly believe that we can accomplish our dreams, or even just get through some of life's most trying times, by always thinking *positively* and having *Faith*. Unfortunately, we have been conditioned to believe that we can't do this or can't do that. If we don't believe in ourselves, no one else will believe in us either. Our mind is a powerful giant within - and without a clear understanding of how it works, we have a difficult time achieving our goals.

You, and only you, can control your destiny. You actively choose to get back up on your feet after difficult times and not just lay down and give up. Your mind is a powerful giant within and your subconscious mind holds the keys to unlock all of your dreams and desires. The more you utilize the great power that your subconscious mind provides, the better your life will be. You have the ability to make decisions that impact your life, so don't wait any longer and start right now to take advantage of the power you have, to make the best decisions.

Even when my husband was going through those terribly dark days, and my own health seemed precarious at best, people asked me how I did it. How did I handle all that stress and trauma? In truth, sometimes I wonder how I did it myself, but I did. I got up every day and got through that day. I couldn't constantly dwell on the "what ifs" or the "maybes". I had to deal with life right then, in the moment and when you do that you will be given strength to persevere.

LESSON # 2

Our thoughts have the power to create a life without limits. Take the time to reprogram any negative thoughts into an encouraging mental support system. Don't lose Faith in God's Power and in yourself.

Chapter 3

Chapter 3

Releasing Anger

I think that I have always had an issue with anger on some level. I tend to hold my emotions inside and when someone does that for long periods of time they will occasionally explode. After Muler's death I was angry. Not at him specifically, but at the circumstances. I didn't understand why my life had to be so hard. Why some people go through so many challenging and devastating circumstances while other people seemed to live happy carefree lives? What did I do to ever deserve this?

As with any issue in your life, in order to really understand the full solution, you must look into the depths of the problem first and that meant looking at my childhood once more.

Growing up, I didn't look for trouble or a fight in school or anywhere else. Having said that, I didn't like to get hurt and if I did, revenge was inevitable. If anybody in school was mean to me or mistreated me in any way, I held on to that grudge until the Friday afternoon. Once Friday arrived, I waited outside the school, and confronted whoever did anything wrong to me during the week.

I remember saying, "Hey you, you messed up with me a couple of day ago, what is your problem? Do you want to fight and settle this now?"

Needless to say this type of confrontation led to many fights during my junior school days. I know some of you may be wondering why Friday, but there was a method to my madness. I chose that day simply because tempers might have cooled off by the next Monday and in some cases, there wouldn't be complaints to the nuns or principals. So I could exact my revenge without paying for it, so to speak.

However, many times when I hurt kids badly (although they were all my age or a little older and I had also been hurt myself), the parents did come to complain on the next Monday – which in turn meant a good beating from the nuns in school and sometimes a message sent to my mom requesting her to come discuss my issues. When Mom was called to school, I was very, very scared. I knew how mad she would be, so I always had a plan to ease her anger.

First, I would start to cry when I am almost a block away from home and as soon as I get home, my mom calmly would ask, "Why are you crying?" This gave me a chance to explain myself.

One example that comes to mind is when I was in Grade 4 and I had a fight with a big girl from Grade 5 who was harassing me and my friends during school recess and lunch breaks. I had to face her on this particular Friday and it took half a dozen people to separate us as she was kicking me with her right hand and foot while both my hands were holding on to her hair pulling her down closer to the floor. Some of her hair came out in my hand!

Of course, her parents showed up at school the following Monday morning demanding that something be done about me. When I went home that day crying, I had to explain to my mom.

I stuttered, "This girl in school was harassing me for so long and I had to face her on Friday. We fought and then I pulled some of her hair and her parents came to school this morning. Then Sora (Sister in Italian) Maria beat me with a stick 30 times in front of my class (I of course had to show the marks on my hand) and now they want you to go to school!"

After hearing such a sob story, she instructed me to clean my face, change clothes and sit down. I did as she said then sat trembling. She always sat cross legged, spoke calmly and stared at me (or anyone who was in the hot seat).

She said, "tell me what happened with the girl, how you say she harassed you and you better tell me everything, in details with no lies as I am going to find out anyway".

I then told her what happened without missing a single detail. Of course it wasn't lies, it couldn't be. You never lied to my mom and she was adamant that you are never ever to lie to anybody about anything.

"Always tell the truth," my mom repeated to both my brother and I constantly during our childhood, even when we were adults.

She also stressed the importance of us looking her in the eye when we talked to her. I know that she demanded truthfulness in part because of her own failures as she had been lied to by my dad, family and some friends on numerous occasions, but still it served us well. This is proof that some of the events in your life can leave you with helpful perceptions and beliefs, while others might be negative.

I inherited this trait of truthfulness from her, Bless her Soul! I never lie and if someone lies to me once, I would be very hard pressed to ever trust them again. I also have a serious problem trusting anyone who cannot look me in the eye. So, after I finished telling my story and she was satisfied with my answers, she then told me to go and do my homework and other tasks before dinner.

The next day, my mom went to school. I have to say that I was very proud of her when she did. My mother was a presence to behold and she naturally commanded the attention of everyone in the room. Even though I knew I was still getting punishment when I got home, the fact that all the nuns were terrified of her, made me feel like a million dollars.

My mom's second language was Italian so she always spoke in Italian with them at the Principal's office. Sometimes, some of my friends would try to pass by the Principal's office in the hope to hear some conversation but they would say, "We can't tell you anything as they are speaking in Italian!"

It didn't matter to me as I knew my mom was totally against harassment and sometimes even against the harsh punishment by the nuns. Her motto was always that it was better if she punished her children than if anyone else does. Not that her punishments weren't just as harsh as the nuns sometimes.

I can honestly say that much of my anger as a child had to do with the harsh punishments handed out by the nuns at my school. Back in those days, it was seen as a good thing to be very harsh to children as that would turn them into good adults, but it traumatized me on many levels and left me with a hatred of authority in certain situations.

When I was in fifth grade, my teacher (a nun) caught me chewing a gum; one of my friends offered it to me and I had forgotten to throw it out before I got to class. The nun called me to come to the front of the classroom, asked me to hand over the gum which I reluctantly did, then made me kneel down on the floor and said to everyone in the class, "Now I am going to teach her the lesson of her life and to all of you too."

She held my head, divided my hair and stuck the gum in the middle of my head and kept on pressing it so hard so that I definitely couldn't get rid of it on my own. That wasn't satisfactory enough for her, so she went brought a wooden broom, and made me get on all fours. She started hitting my back with the broom until the broom was actually broken! She was red with anger and I was in so much pain. The pain was beyond my capability to withstand it yet I did NOT shed a tear. It was all about PRIDE and keeping my head high no matter what was happening. That was also a trait of my mother's.

Crying would have meant giving the nun the satisfaction she needed and I wasn't going to give her that – I would rather die than give her the satisfaction. That was the reason she kept on beating me until the broom broke on my back because I wouldn't cry or scream. The whole class was terrified! I finished the day somehow and wasn't able to carry my backpack as my back was hurting so bad. My friends carried it for me until I got home. I started crying as soon as I walked in the door and mumbled to my mom about what happened to me. I told her about the gum in my hair and about the broom being broken on my back.

My mom checked my hair and froze when she saw what had been done. She told the Nanny to help me get undressed as she wanted to check my back. The Nanny started to cry when she saw my back and shouted for my mom. My mother just stood there like she had been hit with a brick and didn't move. She just stared at my back for what seemed like forever! She then made me lie down in bed and between her and the Nanny, they put ice on my back as I was screaming and crying with pain. Eventually, the ice helped ease the pain. Then it was time to deal with my hair. My mom made me sit on the floor and tried to apply ice on the gum but some of it was impossible to remove. She had no choice but to cut some of my hair.

My hair was my beauty and now, sadly, I had a huge hole in the middle of my hair. My mom had to comb and tie my hair sideways to cover the hole in the middle. I was still waiting for my punishment from my mom. The rule was always if I did something wrong I got punished at school and at home, but not this day. When she was finished, she looked me in the eye and said, "Your punishment from me will have to wait for now as you know very well nobody should chew gum in class. But you are not going to school tomorrow so you can sleep in," then she left the room.

Our wonderful Nanny and I stared at each other and smiled. We were happy that I wasn't going to get any punishment from my mom right then and the fact that I wasn't going to school the next day - yeah! Bonus!

My mom refused dinner that evening and she locked herself in her room. I could tell from her face earlier on that she was fuming! The next morning, she got dressed (looking like a million dollar woman as always) got in her car and was out.

Nanny said to me, "I bet she will go to your school now and swear at all those Italians!"

I smiled at the thought. When she returned, she just checked my back and went to her room. She didn't say anything at all. One of my classmates who didn't live far away from my home came by after school.

She had been hiding by the door so that my mom wouldn't see her and told me, "You should have seen your mom at the Principal's office today! She was banging at their desks and swearing at them in Italian and I know that one word was really bad because my dad uses it all the time when he gets upset!"

Those were the times when I loved my mom the most. So much so that I vowed that I would grow up to be as strong and fearless as she was, but the trauma of repressed anger from ill treatment by the nuns left its mark and I was often given to bouts of rage.

Blinded by Anger

My anger issues didn't go away as I grew. They weren't always as obvious because I had gotten better at hiding them, but that simmering underlying anger lay under the surface of my mind at all times.

In Junior High, I attended a public school rather than the Catholic schools I was used to. One day in eighth grade, a boy sitting behind me, (whom I had been having trouble with for quite a while) decided to call me and my mother a very bad name. I was blinded by an all consuming and sudden rage right in the middle of History class. He whispered his terrible words to me so only the person sitting beside him heard it. All I really remember was standing up, turning around and slapping him so hard on the face that his head snapped back. I then pulled his jacket and tore it from the shoulder down.

Our History teacher, who was writing on the board, turned to look at us after hearing the slapping on the face. Needless to say, he was very shocked and after staring at me and then at the boy for a moment, he ordered both of us to the Principal's office. When the Principal heard the whole story, he had plans for me for the next day.

The very next morning, as the entire school stood in line waiting for the bell to ring, the Principal called my name over the loud speaker. He wanted me to come out in front of everybody. I was shocked and scared and I walked from my line to him at the front. He then announced to the whole school, "This young lady, slapped a young man's face yesterday, and in class. Her punishment for doing that will be to walk on her knees across the school from corner to corner. We will *never* allow a girl to hit a boy! Never! And this should teach all of you girls a lesson!" He then ordered me to get down on my knees and walk across the school yard.

I did what the Principal demanded, and by the time I made it to the other side of the yard, the skin on both my knees was completely ripped off and I was bleeding badly. I could hardly walk. I was so very angry. Not only that he had humiliated me in front of everyone, but that the boy who had started this whole thing went off with no punishment at all. When I was done, I literally crawled to get to the offices. One of the nicer teachers seemed terrified when she saw my bleeding knees and helped me get into one of the offices, sat me down and ran to get some water. She washed my knees and was trembling just at the sight of the damage that had been done. She applied some medicine to my knees and bandaged them very gently. I was in so much pain and yet I did NOT cry! Again, it was all about pride!

The other teachers who saw me were in panic and I actually overheard one of them say to the other "I don't think this guy (the Principal) knows her mom very well! He better be prepared for her as she is going to sue his ass big time!"

Even amidst my pain, I couldn't help but smile and I prayed that my mom would do just that – sue him!

My mom was not a feminist per se but she was very much into women's rights and felt that women, and girls, were to be treated equally and with respect. Needless to say when she saw me, checked my skinless and bloody knees that evening and heard my story as to what happened, what I did and why I was punished, she was livid.

> *Hate cannot drive out hate;*
> *only love can do that.*
>
> *– Martin Luther King, Jr.*

I carried around a very healthy hate for the nuns and their harsh punishments as well as the Principal of my junior high school. I held onto a good deal of anger for them for most of my life and that one incident (along with a few others) really affected the way I viewed the world. I vowed at a young age that I was never to let anyone bully me or hurt me and if someone did, they should pay the price!

It was during a long talk with my mother much later in life when she found out how deeply these incidents had hurt me, not just physically but emotionally. I held on to that hurt and even wallowed in it sometimes as I saw my feelings as justified. It was at that time that my mother sat me down and repeatedly reminded me of the importance of *forgiveness*. I can look back and see that she had made peace with many of the demons in her own life and I needed to do so as well. But it wasn't until I watched the movie The Secret followed by meeting my mentor, Bob Proctor, and many others in the field of personal development, that I learned the importance of releasing past hurts, forgiveness and letting go. It wasn't until then that I actually was able to move beyond my resentments and release that anger I had been building all my life.

The weak can never forgive.
Forgiveness is the attribute of the strong.

– Mahatma Gandhi

Your anger and frustration may differ greatly from mine, but the point is that we all have one thing in common – we have all been angry at one point or another about a circumstance, situation, or event in life. We have all had negative experiences that shaped and skewed our view of the world and we all have people in our lives that need forgiveness.

Even though I suffered terribly in school at the hands of the nuns and chauvinistic principals, the times I was most miserable were the years after the death of Muler. It wasn't until then that all these emotions really came crashing down on me.

I never anticipated being a single mother. It never occurred to me that I could be left on my own to take care of an eight year old through death. *This wasn't how it was supposed to be,* I thought.

I was very angry that I was a single mother because it wasn't in my plan. Muler's death forced me to deal with the reality of raising my son on my own and what that would mean. When people ask me if I was angry that he had died, or angry at God, I told them neither. I wasn't angry at any one person in particular, I was instead angry that the life I had counted on and dreamed of was stolen from me. Or so I thought. It seemed like I was the only one who understood what was going on in my life and knew what I had to deal with. I was just angry, and I wanted my life back the way it was or at least the way I had dreamed it would be. I felt like I somehow lost the right to be happy and secure because it never seemed to happen for me.

As I picked up the pieces of my shattered life and set about raising my son, it became apparent to me that Muler's death brought to the surface so many emotional difficulties that were turning into some serious attitudes. My son started exhibiting anger in an obvious manner that was so unlike him. He lashed out at children in school and talked back to his teachers. He even talked back to me. He took everything people said or did to him very personally. The tears in our home seemed to be flowing day in and day out for more than three years.

On top of this, I had to answer my son's non-stop questions, "Why mom? Why did God have to take my dad away from me? Why?" I just didn't know what to say. I wondered the same thing and I didn't have any answers.

I knew there was probably a reason, but I didn't know what it was. All I could do was get up every day, get through that day and hope the next one was better. So that's what I did.

LESSON #3

Don't waste your life holding onto anger or frustration. Life is too short to try to "right every wrong". Learn to be grateful for the event because out of every bad situation is a lesson.

Chapter 4

Chapter 4

From Fear to Freedom

I can easily say that most people would know what it is like to be unhappy. Many of us could win an Academy Award for our acting abilities each day. We don't want anyone to find out our dirty little secret – that we are angry, terrified, disappointed, or just plain tired of life. We want the outside world to think that we are happy, prosperous and successful, so we act like everything is fabulous. The primary reason we live this great masquerade is because of *fear*. Fear of failure causes many people to never try anything that is not completely safe. So they live their lives full of limitations, never experiencing everything that life has to offer.

Fear of rejection makes us afraid to do anything that could draw criticism or give someone a chance to laugh at us. We are too scared to ask for help, too scared to fail, too scared to look silly or any other fear imaginable. Unhappiness perpetuates fear and fear perpetuates unhappiness so consequently, we end up living in a never ending negative cycle. We all have things that we are afraid of - I was terrified of losing my mother, Muler, and other loved ones - a fear I think we have all had at one time or another about someone close to us and someone we care about.

The Internal War

Fear is a really interesting emotion. It controls so much of our lives on so many levels, but I also think that some of us are more naturally fearful than others. I am one of those people. I guess you could say that I was, and still am, a people pleaser by nature. I want everyone to be happy and I want to do things correctly. I am sure part of that stems from my mother having incredibly high standards for us and I wanted to live up to that expectation. Still, there were times when I felt incredible fear wash over me and this is something I have had to deal with many times.

I think my own fear was a combination of my basic personality and then certain events that took place in my life.

As I stated earlier, when I was a child, we lived in a part of the world not really known for stability (Ethiopia) but it had been peaceful for a while. I had just started Grade Ten and was so excited. I had made many new friends at this time and life was really good.

It was a Friday. My best friend was supposed to come by my house to pick me up so that we could go downtown for a movie. I was getting dressed and looking forward to the evening. My friend and I always had fun and giggled about anything and everything as young girls do.

At this time, my brother had moved back to Sudan after suddenly starting to have a lot of trouble with my mother. He moved and was working in a bank and in a very short period was actually Head of a Department.

My mom was not home at that time or expected back for a few weeks as she had travelled to the province of Tigray, Ethiopia. She had recently found out that she had a few half-brothers that she never knew about. They had come looking for her when they knew they had a half-sister and it was an exciting and emotional time for us all.

Boy, my Grandfather must have been a very busy man – having kids in every province. I thought to myself! After a couple of meetings, they all decided to have a memorial service for their father (the Grandfather I never met as he died long before I was born). So, I was home alone with a cousin who was a little older than me as we didn't have a nanny at this particular time as we were in our mid teens.

It was around 6:30ish pm when the first shots rang out. We had no idea what it was at the time. Apart from watching the movies, we never really saw or heard anybody shooting in real life. We were so very frightened. The shooting went on for less than ten minutes but for us it seemed like a lifetime! Then suddenly, everything went quiet. We could hear people screaming and running around but my cousin and I locked ourselves in my bedroom terrified and crying. When the shooting subsided, we waited a few minutes before coming out of my bedroom. It was a great relief for us to hear our neighbours (over the walls of each side of our house) talking about what just happened. We then decided to peek outside and our street was full of people. The whole neighbourhood was outside discussing this unexpected and terrifying incident!

All this time, I was young and never really listened to, or got involved in, politics but I was hearing bits and pieces of information from my schoolmates and others. I knew that there was some tension going on in the country, in particular, just before Emperor Haile Selassie was toppled from his Kingdom. There were groups against the government of Ethiopia (like freedom fighters) and in particular, Eritreans wanting to have their independence and be separated from Ethiopia. So the shooting was from one of those groups. We all decided this was just a one-time thing, it was over and would probably never happen again.

Awe, I said to myself, *too bad there is no movie now. My friend's parents would never let her leave her home after this incident and neither would my Mom if she was home!* Going out with a friend was about to be the least of my priorities quite soon enough.

A few hours later, the shooting started again. This time there was no stop to it as loads of trucks filled with soldiers were out in the streets of Asmara (capital of Eritrea). Soldiers were shooting at anybody and anything in the way. My cousin and I ran back to my bedroom and sometimes crawled under the bed during some of the attacks. I have never *ever* been so terrified in my life!

I missed my Mom terribly at that moment! I was just a teenager and I so desperately wanted to hear my mother tell me that all would be alright. The news was on the radio as to what was happening by then but my mind was filled with questions, *Would my Mom have heard this news from where she is? And if so, when and how on earth is she going to come back here?* I prayed and cried at the same time.

Mom, I am sorry for all the trouble that I sometimes cause, for being a tomboy or anything you don't approve of, please come back safely here as soon as possible? I cried and prayed.

Beginning from that day and for an entire year, schools were closed. There were no flights, buses or anything for quite some time. There were convoys escorted by soldiers from one city to another or from one province to another. That is if you were lucky and got a spot as tons of people were trying to leave and flee the province of Eritrea as the situation worsened. Expats were transported back to their respective countries through their embassies but everyone else just had to make do. I didn't really sleep and there was constant fear, stress and tension in the air.

The radio was on 24 hours per day and all we heard was lists of those who had died (in particular people in higher positions) and I cried every day, even for the people I didn't know. It was so sad and there didn't seem to be any end in sight. There were huge trucks and soldiers standing on the back of the trucks shooting everywhere including at the houses and windows; basically, at anything they can see. Mostly it was early mornings. At this time, a curfew was announced on radio so that nobody should be out before 6:00 am in the morning or after 6:00 pm in the evening. If you were not home and walking outside during the curfew, you were dead – guaranteed!

For some time, there was no electricity and no water but lucky for us, we had a neighbour across the street who lived in a huge lot that had a well and they allowed us to take water to our home. We all lined up for hours and filled containers for our use, and we had to use what we had very carefully, that included food, candles – everything.

Overcoming my Fear

After the first week of fighting when I had been so terrified and crying almost non-stop, something strange happened to me. I stopped being afraid! I didn't know why or how but I just wasn't afraid anymore. All I remember is that one morning waking up and saying to myself:

"This is obviously going on for a very long time. So why am I so afraid? What is the worst that can happen to me? I will get killed. If I did get killed, then I will no longer have to worry, suffer, and cry for all those dying or anything like that. As a matter of fact, I will be in Heaven living in peace and harmony!"

My cousin that morning was shocked at my sudden change and lack of fear. And when I told her the reasons, she was very confused. I think she thought I was going crazy. It took me a few days of explaining to her (although she was older than me) my point that living in fear wasn't going to change anything!

You gain strength, courage and
confidence by every experience in which
you really stop to look fear in the face.
You are able to say to yourself,
'I have lived through this horror.
I can take the next thing that comes along.'
You must do the thing you think you
cannot do.

– Eleanor Roosevelt

My sense of calm lasted until a huge bullet was shot into my bedroom. That particular day, when the shooting started, we ran and locked ourselves in my bedroom. I sat on the bed – unmoved and unafraid. My cousin begged me to get under the bed but I refused. Finally she forced me to follow her and I went under the bed. A couple of minutes later, we heard a huge sound inside my bedroom almost like a small explosion. My cousin screamed and I just sat there, quietly. I still can't figure out how that big sound inside my room didn't scare me!

I remember thinking to myself death, here you come, just please be quick and painless!

When the shooting subsided after about an hour or so, we came out from under the bed to find a big hole beside my bedroom door and when we looked back following the location it came from, the bullet had landed right on top of my bed! That really scared the crap out of me! If my cousin hadn't forced me to get under the bed, that bullet would probably have shattered my brain! I decided right then and there that I have to listen and be more careful in future but I still insisted that I should NOT be afraid.

"If I die, I die!" I kept on repeating to myself and to my cousin.

By the second week, we started getting water in our home for a couple of hours a day and we got busy filling out every container and every barrel in the house. Electricity also was available for a few hours and that is when we rushed to do our cooking or anything we needed.

It had been two weeks since the war started, when one afternoon there was a knock on the door. My cousin, after making sure it was safe and asking "who is it?" opened the door and there stood my

Mom! She did not say hello but just froze, staring at my cousin. I heard her ask about me and when I came running from my room, I ran to hug my Mom; she was in tears. She held me tight (for the first time as far as I could remember as my Mom was not into hugging and kissing). She then released me and then hugged her niece – all quietly; no words spoken.

Then she did something that I will remember for the rest of my life. She knelt down and kissed the ground repeating "Thank you God, Thank you God, Thank you God!" and her tears flowed.

Her dress was so dirty and her face ashy. I had never, ever seen my Mom like that before. My Mom was the Queen of cleanliness and elegance! She then said, "I need a shower; do we have any water?"

My Mom went to take a shower and I could hardly wait for her to come out. We had so many stories to tell her but more importantly, I was dying to know how she travelled all the way home as there was no formal transportation any longer.

As it turned out, she heard of what happened in Asmara the morning after that Friday night shooting. Just as we did at the beginning, everybody thought that this was a one-time thing and the whole family was waiting for better news on the radio. Of course, it wasn't a one-time incident and the news kept coming on the radio and television.

For my mom to be able to come back to Asmara from Tigray, it would have been a day travel by bus – under normal circumstance that is. But it took her almost two weeks. She had to beg drivers and even soldiers to drop her from one place to another. She slept over at some people's houses (she never knew) along the way. In the cities and towns along the way, people were very helpful and cooperative and they would give the travellers food, water and even a bed for the night. My mom wasn't much of a talker especially with me but that evening after dinner and over a candle she summarized the story for me and my cousin. She also wanted to know every bit of story from us which we quickly shared. Needless to say, her biggest shock was the bullet in my bedroom – on top of my bed!

Then she said something I never expected. She said, "I want you to wake up very early tomorrow morning. I want you to pack a couple of sets of clothes and one pair of shoes each. After breakfast and after the curfew hour is removed, I am going to visit our neighbour (a neighbour who turned out to be more than family) and we will be heading to Tigray. We will not come back here until the war is over."

I could see that my cousin was so happy and relieved – after all, Tigray was where her parents were. For me, however, it was a different story. I was shocked. I wasn't very happy at all. This was where I grew up, this was where all my friends were – even though we weren't able to visit each other since the shooting started but still, this was home and this was where I felt I belonged.

Why should we run away? I thought.

But I never said that out loud. You never asked my mom questions; you just did as she said. So we went to bed with my cousin excited and happy, while I wet my pillow with tears. When I finally fell asleep, I had a nasty and scary dream. All I could see was blood in the streets, on the walls, everywhere.

I was so relieved when my cousin woke me up the next morning – the fact that we were alive and there was no blood in our house made me grateful.

"Thank you God – it was just a dream!" I repeated and rushed to wash up, eat a quick breakfast and pack a few things in a bag.

My mom had already seen our wonderful neighbour and asked her to take care of our house by giving her a spare key we had. She said we would be in touch when the phones started working again. She had already packed water, snacks, a small bag and, of course, some cash.

Then we left. It took us about ten days to get to Tigray. They were adventurous ten days, I can tell you that for sure. But we were lucky and blessed to have arrived in Tigray, safe and sound. We stayed in Tigray Province for the rest of the school year and then we travelled from one city to another as we had family members everywhere. I got used to the circumstances fairly quickly.

Change is not actually a bad thing, I thought. I got to meet so many first cousins and second cousins, some of which I was meeting for the first time.

I missed my friends immensely during this time. Every single day, I thought of my friends, our neighbours, my school mates. I wondered how they were doing and how their families were doing. We listened to the radio and watched TV on a daily basis to keep up with the events. That was a given. When it was news hour, everyone went quiet. You could even hear people breathing as everyone absorbed the latest on Eritrea and in particular Asmara. There was still a little hope for peace in our hearts although the news we heard didn't give any indication that things would ever go back to normal. Meanwhile, I enjoyed my time with family and made new friends. I visited every city in Tigray.

I learned a lot of history from my aunts, uncles, cousins and my new friends. I learned a lot more of the stories of Queen Sheba and King Solomon than I did in school. I learned about the story and the whereabouts of the Ark of Covenant. What an amazing, beautiful and historic country Ethiopia is!

Amidst my new and temporary life that I had begun to enjoy, I cried a lot as I struggled with bouts of sadness and fear. In particular, when I heard the news of so many journalists and high rank people we saw on TV or heard their voices on the radio were announced dead. Not to mention the number of innocent people dying almost every day.

Then there was an announcement on radio and television that was about to change everything, yet again. Schools were closed for the year and new school year was about to begin. It was announced that ALL students MUST return to school. Anyone who didn't register or didn't return, along with their direct families, were to be considered rebels and against the government. I remember looking at my Mom and she stared at me but her eyes were blank. There would be terrible consequences for those that didn't follow the mandate. We didn't talk about it but when my cousins and I left the living room, they asked me if we had to go back. Of course, I didn't know the answer. I also overheard my aunt asking my Mom the same thing.

A few days later, my Mom announced that we were going back for school reasons. By that time, there were convoys of trucks that went from one small city to another and that's how we were to go back which would be a lot easier than the way we came to Tigray. I honestly was happy to go back home. I would finally be able to see my friends and God knows we had a lot of catching up to do! I was also terrified of what lay ahead. As expected, my cousin refused to return with us but who can blame her? So, it was only me and my mom.

The travel back to Asmara was a lot easier this time. We were home within three days. Our neighbours were so happy to see us and it seemed like everybody was crying with happiness. Our neighbours rushed to their homes to bring us food, hot tea, and of course Ethiopian coffee – the best coffee in the world! They also couldn't wait to give us an update of the neighbourhood.

Home sweet home! I can't remember feeling such an excitement for a whole year! I was so grateful to be able to sleep in my own room and in my own bed. Even if the bullet hole was still in the wall above my bed.

My mom and I immediately got busy cleaning our bedrooms and changing the sheets. The rest could wait till the next day. That night, I asked my Mom if I could go visit one particular best friend the next day as they would have no way of knowing that we were back. She told me first we need to get organized and then I could go in a couple of days. She also wanted to change my bed position from where it was before and have the walls repaired properly as the hole by the door was just stuffed to close it temporarily as there was no time for proper repair because we had to leave.

You would think that since I was back to some semblance of normal, that my fear would diminish, but it really didn't. The reason being that now we kept on hearing all the stories of all that had happened to the people we knew.

One of the stories that I will never, ever forget was about a sweet lady who lived a few blocks from us. She owned a variety store and she had two children under the age of twelve. I am not sure if the culprits were thieves or not but she was shot in front of her kids and everything in her store and in her house (they lived at the back of the store) was stolen. Apparently, she told her killers to take anything they wanted and begged them not to hurt her and her children but they still killed her.

Our neighbours told us that the bullet used wasn't from a small gun as most of her organs had fallen out of her body, and the children had to see this. Their father was Italian and in Italy at the time of this horrible incident. The kids were temporarily taken by some family members and then the Italian Embassy immediately flew them to their father. I cried over this story on and off for at least two years - in particular when I passed by their closed store or whenever some neighbour spoke of them. I had nightmares about it for the longest period and this story was just one of many. I am sure that those days I would have been diagnosed with Post Traumatic Stress, but then again, any person who has ever existed in the midst of a war is traumatized.

My best friend froze for what seemed like a long time when she opened the door for me. She then burst into tears and we hugged and cried for a long time. Her mom made us some tea and cookies and left us alone as she knew we had so much to talk about.

Then came the news – one after the other! At least half of the boys in our previous year's class were either found dead or disappeared into thin air. At least 15 of our Junior High School mates had died. Dozens and dozens of our school mates had fled the country, some to Sudan, some to Egypt, some to Kenya – they all fled to neighbouring countries. Every time she mentioned a name and said "died" I cried more.

By the time I had to leave, as I had to be home before the curfew, my eyes were so swollen I could barely see. My mom was shocked when I got home and she sat me down and wanted to know what happened. Between my sobs, I told her about my classmates, and the previous school students. She listened quietly but her silent tears flowed. It could have been us so easily. Mom knew it and so did I.

Eventually, my friend told my other friends of our return and they all came to visit me. More tears and more shocking and sad news was shared as I heard of more people and their family members who either died or vanished.

School finally started and we were happy that the location had changed to a closer one than before. Our original High School was quite a distance and a little out of the city. So many of the children were gone – either having been killed or having fled – that they now combined two schools into one and put us in a central area. Life was beginning to look a little bit more normal.

I will say amongst all the chaos that we had been through, we saw a lot of kindness from people! Neighbours, strangers and anyone would help anyone else in need. In particular, when people were travelling on foot or via convoys.

Even three years after our return from Tigray, there was still a curfew from 7:00 pm until 7:00 am. Any person found walking at any time during the curfew was shot dead – no questions asked. While during the day, life seemed to be normal, there was still a lot of risk and a lot of fear and this permeated every aspect of life.

Things were very, very different. For example, people could not go to a store and buy basic flour, sugar and so many other items. Families were registered in their individual communities and received a portion of everything according to the number of people per household. There was always a long line just to get a kilogram of sugar or flour.

There was also a lot of harassment in the streets. Walking to school and back was not always safe and as much as possible, those who lived in the same area walked together. I faced so many harassments and threats from some of the Navy, Police, and other so called powerful people. I felt my life was always in danger – and it was.

It was at this point that my mom decided that this was enough and it was time for us now to immediately find a way to go back to Sudan. She said if we stayed, I would either be jailed, abused or killed as so many young women were. This time however, leaving Asmara was going to be for good.

The trip from Asmara to Sudan took 19 days and what we faced in those 19 days is definitely another book by itself!

I can look back on this period in my early to late teen years and see how much living in constant fear affected me although I tried to fight it time and time again. It was completely out of my control and I didn't like not having control. The feeling of being out of control is where a lot of unhappiness, fear and anger came from in my life. I felt as if life was happening to me, instead of having any sort of choice in the matter. This meant fear was my constant companion and never completely left.

Even years later when I thought I had gotten my life in order, Muler's battle with cancer once again opened all these old wounds. I didn't have control of the situation. There wasn't anything I could do to make it better or change the outcome and it meant that the grand dreams I had for my life were not going to happen as I envisioned. But I also knew that I was becoming strong and resilient. I was flexible and accepting of change more so than ever before and somehow I knew that my future would be bright and full of hope.

LESSON #4

Fear prevents you from accomplishing your dreams. Have faith and move forward knowing that the best is yet to come.

Chapter 5

Chapter 5

Intuitiveness

People have told me that I have a keen intuition and I know that it is true. I can sense people's true intentions and often I get a sense for which direction I must go simply by listening to that small still voice inside myself. I can think back and point to specific events that solidified this intuition and helped me learn to listen to these clues about people and events.

I always loved people. As a kid, I was the first to run and open the door when the bell rang or I heard a knock. I was happy having visitors which were mostly my Mom's friends or family members. I would hug them with a huge smile on my face - with the exception of this one particular woman. I was about 11 years old and this woman seemed to visit our home mainly for my Mom, but I never hugged her. There was this off putting aura about her. Having said that, at the time, I didn't even know what the word aura meant and neither did I hear about it. But for some bizarre reason, I couldn't stand her. She would pull me to kiss my cheeks and I would wipe my face and go sit in my room and mumble "I don't like that woman".

Once our Nanny asked me "why is she so different to you that you don't run hug her like you do with other people, what did she do to you?"

"Nothing - but there is something about her that is not good – I know it," I replied and she laughed.

I also noticed that my Mom was colder toward her than she usually was with people but this woman never got the message and kept coming back uninvited and unwanted. She would always look around the house as if trying to see if there was something new in our home or as if she was sizing up our possessions which I found disturbing and strange. She never looked you in the eye when she spoke to you either, which my mother had taught me was a trait of dishonesty. She also constantly complained about my mother's dog. My Mom loved dogs and we always had one growing up. Our dog at the time didn't seem to like this woman and he wouldn't stop barking from the time she walked in until she left! It was very strange as he never did that with other visitors. That made the two of us who didn't want her to visit though I am sure my mother wasn't thrilled to see her either.

On one particular visit, she asked my Mom angrily, "Roma, why do you always have to have a dog in this house?"

My Mom looked coldly at this woman's face and in a low but very firm tone replied "Because dogs are more faithful to their families and friends than some human beings are".

The Nanny and I were shocked but nothing compared to this woman's shock. Looking at her face was priceless to me. "God, I love my Mom!" I said quietly to myself!

As it turned out, a short time later our dog was unleashed and playing with me in the yard when this same strange woman knocked on the door. I opened it and our dog darted in, catching the fabric of her dress, tearing it apart! My Mom told him to stop and while he normally obeyed and listened, he did not on this particular day! The woman screamed and ran out the door. I couldn't have been happier and was surprised to see the smirk on my Mom's face as well as the fact that she wasn't upset with our dog. The woman never came back, but I didn't mind. I knew there was something not right about her. Later on, we heard horror stories about this woman and how she hurt people and lied to everyone and even had couples get into a fight because she stirred up so much trouble.

At the time I didn't know my ability to discern good or bad in others was called 'intuition'. But I could always tell someone's heart by looking into their eyes and having a short conversation.

"How did you know and how do you know these things and why is it you always seem to be right?" My best friend complained to me one day when we were in our twenties.

"I'm not sure, but I know and I can feel it," I replied to her after she broke up with a boyfriend she had dated for a short period. We met this guy together and in about ten minutes or so, I decided I didn't trust him. My friend however, really liked him (he was a charmer and very good looking - to give him some credit) and went out on a date with him declining all my warnings and advice. A few months later, she came to me crying and telling me how he lied to her and that he was seeing this other girl for a few years therefore he was using her. That is when she asked how I knew he was untrustworthy.

Intuition isn't some special gift that some people have and others don't. We all have intuition. Have you ever had a hunch or inspiration about something? Have you ever walked into a room and you just knew that something isn't quite right? That is your intuition speaking. We can all improve our intuition just by practicing and you are never too old to learn!

> *Intuition is the faculty of knowing before you think.*
>
> *–John Assaraf*

Intuition is the still, small voice that speaks to each of us and guides us, if we let it. As I have come to learn, contrary to popular belief, we are not physical beings having a spiritual experience; we are spiritual beings having a physical experience. We have a physical body, but we aren't our body. It is the spirit inside of us that is who we are and our bodies are mere extensions of that spirit. Our five senses are what help us interact with the world around us. They are our antenna to receive information from the external world. Our intuition, on the other hand, is our direct line to the spiritual side of our natures.

How Does Your Intuition Talk to You?

Most often your intuition will communicate with you in a small, quiet way. Here are a few examples to give you an idea of how your intuition talks to you.

1. When you are walking to your car in a dark parking lot at night and suddenly the hairs on your neck stand on end.

2. You go to a party and meet someone who just gave you a "bad vibe." You were completely uncomfortable around this person even though you had no logical reason to feel this way.

3. When your spouse comes home from work after a particularly rough day and you can just feel his/her bad mood as soon as they walk through the door.

4. A sickening feeling in the pit of your gut that something is wrong with a friend or family member you haven't seen in a while.

5. The first answer you feel prompted to select when taking a test. Most of the time, we will change that first answer and when we get our test back, we see that our first instinct was correct and the answer we reasoned to be the best was incorrect.

Ignoring our Intuition

Sadly, few people actually listen to that internal voice of infinite knowledge and wisdom. Why do we ignore such a valuable counselor and guide in our lives? At best, as we are growing up, we are taught to ignore our intuition – at worst, we are taught to completely distrust it. I had a very strong feeling that something more serious was wrong with Muler about his stomach pains which is why I nagged him to insist on more tests. My suspicion (or should I call it my gut feeling?) was right and though he received a terrible diagnosis, it would have been much worse if he had just suddenly died and we didn't get those last couple of years with him.

In much of Western Society, we are taught to make decisions based on what we can see, smell, taste, touch, and hear. Intuition is none of those things; therefore, we determine it must not be real, or at least not a reliable way by which to make decisions. We use our faculty of reason and determine that intuition cannot be detected with our five senses, therefore it must not exist.

Well, our intuition is the main tool we can use to tap into information that surrounds us that exists on a level that we can't see with our physical eyes. We can't see the hunches or intuitive nudges. We can't see the impression we get that tells us to do things at a certain time, for example, to call a friend you haven't spoken with for a while.

We can't see the nudge that tells us to take our umbrella with us even though the skies are clear. We can't see the foreboding feelings that prompt us to know something is not quite right. Yet, deep inside we can feel all of these things. We must begin to recognize that our spiritual factors are every bit as real as our sensory factors and need to be exercised to be fully functional.

Have you ever felt that you were pressured to do something or go somewhere and you didn't want to, but end up going anyway to please your friends or family? And then something really goes wrong? Yes, it has happened to me a few times in my lifetime – NOT ANYMORE!

I always really loved dancing and this used to be my weekend treat. Going dancing with my friends and/or cousins every Friday night where there were good and high-end discos and I loved it.

One weekend however, I had this knot in my stomach every time I thought about going dancing and I told my friend it was better if we took it easy that night, and may be watch a movie or something. She wouldn't take no for an answer. I even told her she could go with the rest of the group and I can stay home and read a book.

"You and your freaking books." She said, "You have plenty of time during the week to read and since when do you say no to dancing anyway? What is wrong with you?"

She called some of our group and they came to my home to pick me up. I gave in and got ready and went with them. Well, that night ended up being quite a nightmare, to say the least. A huge fight erupted at the dance floor that took a lot of people to break up and it was just a horrible night.

Once again, later on, I was pressured to go to a party but didn't feel like it, and another huge fight broke out between my cousin and some guy who asked me to dance, twice. Our dancing party was cut short and we had to leave early. I was happy to be home. I then swore to myself, and told my friend, that I will never go anywhere again if I have that bad feeling. And I will never be convinced by anyone to change my mind. I decided at the time that I wasn't going to give in to anybody or try to make anyone else happy if I didn't have a good feeling! What is wrong with staying home, spending time with family and may be read a good book? Especially, if something inside you is telling you "don't do it"?

Intuition plays a big part in our decision making. Ultimately, you are the best person to make decisions in your life. Rather than seeking approval from others around us for decisions we are contemplating, we should turn inward and seek guidance from our intuition.

Again, there is great power in asking questions and this will help to invoke your intuition. When making decisions pepper yourself with questions. What is it you are making a decision about? How do you feel about the situation? What are some possible outcomes of the decision? After you ask the questions, it is time to **listen** for answers.

Listen to Your Dreams

Another way our intuition can speak to us is through our dreams. Very often, our dreams contain messages and insights for us. Sometimes, I wake up so happy and I don't know why. If the feeling continues, I always receive a surprise. "I am going to hear something good today – I know it!" I say to myself and in most cases it happens. Most of my cousins and my best friends are now scattered around the world from Ethiopia to the Middle East, to England, to Germany, to Italy, to Switzerland, to Germany, USA and some still in Sudan. So when I have one of those good feelings, I normally receive a call or an email from one of them or hear some good news about someone and sometimes it would be something to do with me personally.

There was another time that a dream I had gave me direction. It was in the mid eighties in Khartoum, Sudan. I was very sick and left work early. And since my Mom was in Ethiopia visiting her family at the time, my friend insisted taking me home with her that afternoon. Her Mom was one of the sweetest human beings and she had prepared soup and a lot of healthy food for me. After taking some medication, the Mom took me to my one of the bedrooms and told me to rest. I was fast asleep even though it was late afternoon.

I dreamt that I was on a long street, long white walls lined on both sides of the street – no houses, no trees, nothing. I was standing there with a couple of packed suitcases that were really heavy, waiting for a bus. Not too far from me was someone I really loved and respected along with a couple of other people. I won't mention the name but this someone was staring at me in a very weird way with a mysterious smile on their face. I couldn't stop staring back wondering why this someone was alongside those other people instead of being by my side and trying to help me with my suitcases. The bus arrived and that someone along with their new found friends got on the bus without asking me if I needed help getting the heavy suitcases on the bus and actually looked back at me smiling. The bus took off leaving me and my luggage there – all alone in this huge street where there was nobody else left.

I sat on top of one of the suitcases and cried. I cried as to how on earth I was going to get home and most importantly, I cried for the person I thought was a good and loyal friend when suddenly a huge green window opened up in the wall behind me, terrifying the heck out of me and interrupting my tears! In the window, a beautiful lady with a beautiful smile wearing a white scarf, a white top with light blue flowers appeared. After staring at her for what seemed like a lifetime I managed to open my mouth and ask, "Who are you? Where did you come from? There was no window up until a few minutes ago!"

She slowly said, "It doesn't really matter who I am or where I came from, what is important is that I am here and I am here to help you."

With that I woke up from my deep sleep – sweating head to toe and my heart pounding. I shouted for my friend and her lovely Mom and told them my dream and the Mom was in shock and kept repeating "In the Name of the Father, the Son and the Holy Spirit" over and over again and for a minute I thought she hadn't heard me properly.

After gathering herself together she said to me (and of course my friend), "Get ready. We have to go to St. Mary's Church – because that lady you saw is Mary!"

I was dumb founded but I followed her orders. We went to St. Mary's Church (on the way she stopped us by a store and bought two boxes of candles) and she made me light up a dozen candles, pray and thank her (St. Mary) for appearing in my life and for helping me. I did everything (although I have to say, I was a little hesitant at the time) she told me to.

Not long after this dream and experience, that special person in my dream did exactly what I **saw** in my dream. I was going through a rough personal time and that person decided to look the other way. Completely acting as if I was someone they hardly knew. It hurt. It hurt a lot! We didn't speak for so many years after that. And just like in my dream, I have always been lucky and had good people around me. People, who would do anything for me, guide and support me. The support may not have come directly from a woman who looked like St. Mary, or the woman by the window that I saw in my dreams, but I am sure she was part of all my solutions.

That same woman (or should I call her St. Mary) has come to me in my dreams three times since then – through the same window. Same top, same scarf and same smile!

I also have bad and scary dreams from time to time that cause me to wake up sweating with my heart pounding so hard and loud that I would think it might jump from my chest. I have learned now that it always means less than good news is on the way. It is a way of preparing me in advance.

It was in the middle of October 1995 when I had one of those bad dreams. My Mom was in Addis Ababa, Ethiopia at the time and I was still working in Abu Dhabi, United Arab Emirates. I was trying to get her a Visa so she could visit and spend a couple of months with me.

But personally applying for a visit visa for my mom at that particular time wasn't easy for me due to the political environment following Iraq's attack on Kuwait in 1990. This meant that some of the neighbouring countries were on the bad side of the Middle East countries and UAE to be specific (at least, that is what I knew as I lived there). One of these countries that was condemned for supporting Saddam Hussain during his Kuwait invasion was Sudan. So my holding a Sudanese passport didn't make my life any easier and therefore, I wasn't able to get my application for my mom's Visa application to be accepted.

One of my close friends, Manal, who had some connections finally managed to help get the Visa for my Mom and this obviously called for a celebration! So, my best friends, Diana, Haifa, Nagwa, Nina, Manal, Khawla and I decided to go out and celebrate. But deep inside, I didn't feel the happiness as much as I should have even though I tried. I couldn't get rid of the sadness that I felt since the bad dream that I had. I even told my friends and my cousin Dina that I didn't know what it was - but I had this bad feeling. They all shrugged it off and told me that everything was going to be fine.

It was a day or two later that I called my Mom. It was a Friday (I always called her every week at the same day and at the same time), and as it turned out she wasn't able to speak to me on the phone. One of my aunts told me that my Mom wasn't feeling well and kept on asking about me.

This annoyed me and I yelled, "put my Mom on the phone right now!"

Then another older aunt took the phone and told me that my Mom wasn't able to speak to me. She was very weak and her voice was very low and they themselves couldn't even hear her! By this time, I was crying and it only got worse for me when my aunt said, "if you can, it is best that you come here right away!"

"How could something like that happen in just 6 or 7 days? I spoke to her last Friday and she was fine and I was happy and couldn't wait now to give her the good news that I have a Visa for her to come visit me?" I said to my aunt.

She replied that it wasn't possible for her to fly anywhere in her current condition. I asked them hundreds of questions as to whether they took her to a doctor, what her illness was and so forth, but the doctor said after seeing both her feet swollen, that there was nothing he could do for her and that they should take her home. I cried and cried. I then called my friend Diana immediately followed by a call to my cousin Dina. They both came running to my home to console me.

Of course, I couldn't fly to Ethiopia so easily either! I was born in Sudan and held a Sudanese Passport. My mom was Ethiopian.

To add to my dilemma, Ethiopia and Sudan were also involved in major political tension at the time. Egyptian President, Hosni Mubarak was visiting Addis Ababa for an African Summit, OAU to be specific when some people tried to assassinate him. He was saved and returned back to Cairo immediately. After a few days, we heard that Ethiopia was accusing Sudan of having a hand in trying to assassinate President Mubarak. Before this incident, Ethiopians didn't require visas to visit Sudan and Sudanese people didn't need one to visit Ethiopia. This was no longer the case which meant I needed a Visa to go to Ethiopia to visit my own mother. I called the closest Ethiopian Embassy which was in Saudi Arabia and they asked for documentation including proof that Roma was actually my mother (e.g. Birth Certificate) and they told me that it could take at least two weeks!

Unfortunately, my Mom didn't wait for me. I called my aunts twice per day and that particular morning, October 22nd, 1995, my aunt asked me "can you come today?"

I was thinking "what is wrong with these people! Don't they get it? That I am having difficulty just trying to get myself a visa?"

I was getting angrier and angrier at my aunts and cousins because I didn't seem to be getting a straight answer about my Mom. I replied to my aunt that I couldn't and need two or three more days until I received a fax with a copy of my Visa and then she added "can you come tomorrow?"

A good friend had a connection with the Ethiopian Airlines Regional Director had managed to get me a visa much faster than the embassy would have, which still needed two or three more days. I was getting more ticked off by the minute with my aunt on the phone, "isn't she listening to me?" and I told her I couldn't be there the next day either.

Apparently, my Mom passed away during my call and her last words that were whispered to my aunts were, "don't scare her, she wouldn't be able to handle seeing me like this" and she was gone. They told me all this and so much more after I finally made it to Addis Ababa.

It is a tradition in the Ethiopian culture that you never tell someone this kind of news in the middle of the day or over the phone. So, at 6:00 am the next morning, my cousin Dina showed up. I was shocked to see her so early in the morning (I was already up, showered and was brushing my teeth) and still didn't get the message. Did she have an argument with her husband? was the first question that went through my mind until I came out to the living room and saw my all my best friends following her - mostly dressed in black.

That's when I got the message even without any of them opening their mouth and I fell to the floor screaming, "Why, God, Why? Why couldn't you let her wait for me? I would have wanted to hear her last words? Why? Why?" To make things worse, half an hour later I found out that my Mom was buried that morning! A day after she passed. I was devastated.

At the time, they didn't have a refrigeration system for dead bodies and burial had to take place within a day or two maximum which is why my aunts kept asking if I could come the next day. This news that my mother had already been buried to me was almost as bad as the loss itself. My Mom's funeral took place with **none** of her children present. She had two of them for heaven's sake! I was upset, angry, frustrated and grieving.

"I am going to Canada as soon as all this is over!" I swore to myself. In my mind, Canada was the land of opportunity. No more of this political ridiculousness! I would not want to ever live in a country that prevented me from hearing my own mother's last words! I finally managed to get to Ethiopia a few days after the funeral and most of the family were at the Airport waiting for me. I told them that they should take me to the cemetery first which they did. I wept uncontrollably and they literally had to carry me to the house where my Mom lived.

I stayed in Addis Ababa for about two weeks. I got rid of furniture and packed all her personal belongings and brought some with me. I left enough money with one of my aunts for the family to build a beautiful monument for my Mom and for a decent memorial service on Day 40 of her passing – a tradition.

My best friends were waiting for me at the Dubai Airport. They didn't take me to my place and instead took me to one of their homes. God Bless them all – my best friends. How much I love and miss each and every one of them!

I think my mother's death and my frustration in not being able to be there was fortuitous in a way. Had it not happened that way I may not have decided to come to Canada and my life may have been much more tumultuous. But that voice of intuition knew it was the right decision and in 1997, that is exactly what I did. I immigrated to Canada and became a Canadian citizen three years later.

When you are able to listen to that still small voice, and develop a strong relationship with the part of you that holds infinite wisdom, it will never lead you astray. You will have a mighty fine captain help guiding you through life's occasional rough waters in the sea of life. Your intuition will help you find direction during the tumultuous, stormy nights and keep you on course during the calm, sunny days.

As you strengthen your intuition and act on the hunches you receive, you will access your infinite potential and you will begin to live a fuller, richer, more abundant life in every aspect of your life.

LESSON #5

- Listen to your inner voice, your gut feeling.
- Your intuitiveness never lies to you.
- Follow it.

Chapter 6

Chapter 6

Health

I know it may seem a bit strange to have a chapter about health right in the middle of my memoir, but I truly believe that every experience we have offers us a chance to learn life lessons. The experience of Muler's illness, and subsequent death, gave me a whole new awareness about the role health plays in a person's well being. We often don't realize that our negative feelings are exacerbated by how we feel and taking care of ourselves while in the midst of crisis is critical in keeping a positive attitude. I know these things personally not only from having witnessed Muler's struggle, but because I did not take care of myself as I should have during that time. My own health diminished and it is impossible to be a caretaker and not take care of yourself. You will burn out quickly.

Muler's chemotherapy treatment was a large dose taken twenty four hours a day for seven days a week. Due to this large dose, he had to go to the hospital for a weekly chemotherapy refill as well as a blood test. We were advised that there would be unpleasant side effects, as well as what he should eat, and what to avoid. They handed us booklets full of information. This was the first time the seriousness and reality of this nasty disease hit the both of us and to say we were unprepared was an understatement.

After all arrangements were made, Muler asked the doctor, "How long do you believe I can I live with this treatment?"

She told him if his body tolerates the treatment, he may live for about two years. It was crushing to a man with a young child. That's when he cried for the first time ever in front of me, and for the last. I cried too but for me it wasn't the first time and wasn't the last either.

After we cried together, he said, "My son is only six years old you know, does this mean I won't be able to see him grow?"

She was so quiet and her face was red. Finally she tapped him on his shoulder and said, "I know, I have a six year old daughter too."

It wasn't long until Muler had to quit his job due to the extensive cancer treatment. His inability to work took a toll on our finances and this added another layer to an impossibly stressful situation. He was in a new job and on a probation period of three months before he received full benefits from the company. We had no medical, no insurance and no short or long term disability benefits from his job available to help us through this situation. It was mentally and physically exhausting.

Chemotherapy is something I would never, **ever**, wish for anyone! It almost killed him before the cancer did. He was attacked by the worst side effects I could have imagined and even the medical staff told us they were unusually severe. So many times, different unexpected side effects presented themselves which forced me to pick up the phone and call the emergency line at the hospital and tell them exactly what was happening; they would then advise me to bring him to emergency immediately. Usually they would stop the chemo for a few days only to resume when the side effects subsided.

After almost four months of intense chemotherapy, vomiting day and night, a loss of at least 40 pounds, complete hair loss and so many emergency calls and sleepless nights, Muler's body couldn't take any more of the chemo. After he stopped the treatment, a blood test indicated that this harsh treatment did destroy about fifty percent of the cancer cells. This news brought us a renewed hope. Though he wasn't able to take any more treatment for a couple of months, this pause in treatment enabled him regain a little bit of his health and immune system somewhat so he would be strong enough to undergo surgery to remove half his stomach and half his liver.

During the time of his chemotherapy (and the years to follow prior to his death), I was only sleeping an average of about three hours a night. Between the midnight medication doses, helping him when he was nauseated during the night and waking up early to get both him and my son ready for the day, I was exhausted. Not only was I taking care of Muler, my son Michael needed me too. After preparing breakfast and getting the medications for the day, I helped Michael get ready, dropped him off at daycare and then hit the hour long commute to work. On top of all of this stress, I had to deal with my own Type 2 Diabetes.

Most days, I picked up a bagel for breakfast on the way to work. I didn't have much of an appetite, so I skipped lunch often. I knew well enough that skipping meals was definitely not what someone with diabetes should do - under any circumstances. And yet, it was very difficult for me to eat proper meals with all the stress and anxiety. I had no appetite. My wonderful colleagues and friends at work begged me to go to lunch with them or at least asked to pick me up something on their way back almost every day. They were all worried about me and my health. After work, I would pick up Michael from daycare and as soon as we got home, I would check on Muler and his immediate needs. I then fed Michael his dinner. After allowing him to do his homework and watch a little TV, it was then time for his bath followed by reading in bed until he fell asleep. Then it was time to prepare for what was needed the next day. Meals for Muler, medications for the night, Michael's clothes for the next morning and so forth.

When it was time for me, which was rare, I was so wiped out that I couldn't care less about food or exercise or anything else really. However, I usually did manage to eat yogurt or a banana in the evening. Both of which didn't require a lot of chewing, were easy to swallow and in my mind, still considered good enough to take my evening diabetes medication. Needless to say, I started to lose weight very quickly and my hair fell out by the handful due to the stress.

The Big Day – The Surgery

The day of Muler's surgery, we arrived at the hospital around six in the morning. I prayed constantly. By the afternoon, a few friends, some family and I sat waiting and we watched different doctors and surgeons coming out to other parents or family members saying "congratulations, the surgery was successful." I smiled and thanked God knowing that the worried people heard good news and prayed I would hear the same.

Remember the phrase, when it rains it pours? We were one of the two last families sitting there waiting for someone to come out and give us good news when Muler's surgeon stormed out of the doors and walked toward us. My heart pounded and I was having trouble breathing. My intuition knew that it was bad. I recognized that same expression from January 2006 when he gave us the news that the cancer had spread from Muler's stomach to his liver. Now the doctor sat across from me in the waiting area, looked me in the eye and said, "I am so sorry to have to tell you this but we didn't do the surgery".

It took me a few seconds to absorb what I just heard, I finally managed to say, "what where you doing all day long then - and why not?"

He took a deep breath and said to me "unfortunately when we opened him up, we found out that the cancer cells had multiplied and spread everywhere".

I cried and so did all our friends – men and women both.

The surgeon sat there repeating, "I am sorry. I am so very sorry".

After a few minutes I managed to say to him "why didn't you just go ahead and do it anyway and may be with more treatment and radiation, it would have helped?"

He said, "that would have meant removing half of all his organs and it just wasn't possible". I continued to cry for what seemed forever and the doctor respectfully remained seated until my crying subsided.

I managed to ask him if Muler knew the result of the failed surgery and the answer was that he didn't know as he was still asleep and wouldn't wake up until late evening at which time he would be transferred to another part of the hospital. The doctor told me that he asked the nurses to call him when Muler woke up so he could deliver the bad news. At that moment, I got up and left the room to go outside as I felt I was going to die right there and then if I didn't go out where there was some fresh air for me to breathe. I didn't even say anything more to the doctor.

A couple of our friends followed me outside. This whole turn of events took a while to absorb and by this time I was more worried about the reaction of Muler when he discovered the results. This was a death sentence killing any hope he would have had. He would be devastated, as I was, as we all were.

Dear God, why, why, why? For heaven's sake, he tolerated all the nasty treatments and never gave up hope - so why? He was so hopeful that this was to be a success and that he will live long enough to see his son off to University, he would even have been happier to see his son off to high school only - so why? No answer. Or if there was an answer, I was too upset to hear it.

Muler finally woke up late in the evening. He was smiling and the first thing he asked, "was I brave? – did I do a good job?"

Some of us had to run out to cry! Nobody would or could say a word. One of the nurses informed the surgeon and he quickly arrived accompanied by another doctor. They slowly told him the truth. Muler was quiet for about a minute or longer and just stared at the doctor. He was in shock and in a quick flash of anger he told the doctors to just leave.

The surgeon repeated, "I am so sorry, we have tried our best, I am sorry."

Muler went blank for it seemed like the longest time while his brother and our friends, along with me, cried. He didn't show any sort of reaction we were anticipating. After a very long awkward silence he softy said to us, "that's it then, I am done".

All his friends quickly told him not to lose hope and not to lose faith. He looked at everyone like they were crazy and completely out of their minds. He didn't need to say anything further as I knew the look he gave us meant, "it's over and please shut up!".

Natural/Alternative Medicine

I don't think I ate or drank much at all directly prior, and for the few days after the failed surgery. It was as if hope was the only thing sustaining me and now that, too, had been taken away. Muler had to stay in the hospital for a few more days to make sure he didn't get any sort of infection from the surgery attempt. When the doctors approved him to go home, he was happy, very happy, just to be free from being poked and prodded on an hourly basis.

While Muler recovered from the surgery and rested at home, one of his close friends, Woldu, visited one morning and mentioned to us about a Chinese gentleman who was apparently well known in the Toronto area. He treated many types of diseases and suggested that we should give his methods a try. At this point, there was no reason not to as everything else had failed.

We scheduled time and Woldu took us to visit this man. It was a long wait but when it was our turn, the old gentleman checked Muler and told him that it was possible he could be helped/treated. He prescribed some traditional medicines, mostly drinks that would help Muler regain his strength. This treatment was extremely pricey so I took a loan to purchase a one month supply. We had no clue as to how on earth we were going to afford the next month's treatment but Muler's brothers, Berhane from Toronto and Dawit (who lived in Washington at the time but currently resides in Los Angeles), paid for the following two months. It was wonderful that they helped us but I still had no clue how we were going to pay for the months to come!

By this time however, my own health had really taken a blow. I was tired all the time and it seemed as if I was just going through the motions of life. I couldn't take any more worry about what might, or might not, happen. I needed to focus on each new day as it came because worrying about what might happen tomorrow was only doing me more damage.

When some of the family members, and all our friends, heard about this new traditional treatment, they surprised us by contributing money enough to last a good six months! I can't begin to tell you how surprised and touched we were at this response and more than that, how grateful we were! These people are people I will never ever forget– family and friends. It gave us that little shred of hope to keep holding on. We knew that Muler's time would be limited, but each day with our son was priceless for them both so having a chance to extend that time by days, months or even years was worth the price.

The natural treatment by this old Chinese gentleman helped Muler tremendously! As nasty tasting as these drinks were - with a nasty smell, we saw him start to put on some weight each week, his hair grew and he gained some energy which he had had virtually none of while undergoing chemo. He even started to help me by dropping off and picking up Michael at school. It was like a miracle! For a few more months, we were living in bliss as it seemed he was improving and our hope grew each day. That is, until we heard back from the Princess Margaret Hospital where he underwent all his chemo treatments.

We received the much dreaded call from the hospital that it was time for Muler to start chemotherapy again. I was shocked and told the senior nurse that he was taking natural medicine and had improved a lot; definitely more than when he was on chemotherapy. I questioned why he needed more chemotherapy now as it seemed to have done little for him thus far. Her answer was that they don't deal with natural medications, and though they may seem to help, they tend to wreck the blood. She scheduled an appointment for us to go see the chemo doctor the following week.

My intuition told me to just ignore this more chemo treatment request and just focus on the alternative treatment. I knew that more chemo would kill him, but I couldn't make that decision. Muler had to decide whether he should be going back to chemo or just continue with the alternative treatment. He really liked his chemo doctor and said we should go and discuss the options with her - which we did. Their advice was that he could do both chemo and alternative treatment if his body could take it, by only stopping the alternative treatment for the chemo one day before and one day after. Muler agreed to do both. I didn't want him to do chemo again at all as the alternative medicine was working well for him but there was nothing I could do. Yet again, my instinct was right because as it turned out, he could no longer take the alternative medicine along with the chemo treatment. He simply couldn't stand the taste or the smell of his natural medication while taking chemo. He did try his best for the first few days but would immediately run to the washroom to throw it up.

About a month after he re-started chemotherapy, I was flipping channels on TV just to check the weather for the next day when I saw an interview with Dr. Deepak Chopra. I have been, and will always be, a huge fan of Deepak, so I watched the interview. The subject of the interview took me by complete surprise.

He was discussing cancer and alternative treatment! Is it because I have been thinking about this subject quite a lot lately that it showed up on TV and with Deepak Chopra? I think it was Devine intervention somehow.

I hadn't heard the original question but whatever he was asked, Deepak's response and the timing shocked the heck out of me! He was saying "he doesn't believe in chemotherapy" and when asked "why and what should cancer patients do then" his answer was "chemotherapy makes the cancer cells angrier and then they multiply and that people should consider natural/alternative treatment". I shouted for Muler to come watch that and he was equally shocked and told me "you knew it too, I guess as I could see it in your face that you didn't want me to go back to chemo!" This was true, but I knew he had to come to this understanding himself. I couldn't do it for him.

By the time the second round of chemo treatment duration was over, Muler decided that he now had to go back to the Chinese gentleman for more alternative treatment. The reaction he got was totally unexpected. The old man looked, checked his eyes, his tongue and was mad as hell!

He asked, "Why you stop my treatment and why you go back to chemo! You spoiled everything that was going right for you!"

Oh Lord, please no more bad news and no more disappointments, please, please dear God, I can't handle it? I prayed to God silently.

The old man paced around the room fuming and it took him a little while to calm down a little. He then softy said, "You can try to take the medicine all over again, but I don't think it will help as much as the first time. All we have to do is keep on trying."

Another blow for us! How many of these blows were we going to be able to handle? I wondered, is it ever going to turn around and change at some point or at any time at all? God, please, any miracle would help, please, I prayed.

One evening right after our second visit with the Chinese gentleman, Muler received a call from an old friend who lived in the United States. He shared with him a story of a girl he personally knew that was paralyzed and in wheelchair whose doctors tried everything but lost hope on her. This girl was sent to this apparently well-known clinic in Mexico where she was treated by alternative medicine, and was now completely recovered, out of the wheelchair, able to walk, work and lead a very normal life. He strongly suggested that we check it out and give them a call and try their treatment. He provided the contact numbers and address.

The next morning I got busy contacting the clinic explaining Muler's illness and current situation; and I got all the necessary information required for him to visit them. We had to have him try. It was our last resort and our last hope. I made all the flight and hotel arrangements for him. Both my brothers-in-law offered to go with him but he flat out refused to let any of them, or anyone else accompany him.

"It is unnecessary, more expense and it is only for two nights. I promise to call you and update you every step of the way so I don't want you to worry," he said to us.

The clinic advised us that every patient stays at a certain hotel in San Diego, and then fasts for 12 hours before the day the patient is going to meet with the doctors. A bus would pick up all the patients from the hotel early in the morning and drive them to the clinic in Mexico. To his amazement, Muler met so many Hollywood film directors, a bunch of wealthy people and even some doctors who brought their wives or a family member to this clinic. I remember thinking that if other doctors sent their loved ones to this clinic then it had to be something special.

This was a clinic with real oncology doctors but unlike traditional oncologists, they treated patients with natural/alternative medicine only. Muler spent one day full of testing and was given so many types of natural medication and a list of vitamins that he should be taking. The vitamins were prescribed to him by brand name and from certain manufacturers. They could only be purchased from a natural health stores – not from drug stores. They advised him that they would call him within a week with the test results and next steps.

A week went buy and as promised, we received a call from the oncologist who saw him in Mexico. The conversation took a turn for the worse when the doctor said, "The number of your cancer cell count is extremely high. We only wish you had come to us as soon as you found out or at least a few months earlier, but please keep taking the medications we gave you as instructed along with the vitamins. It is a long shot, but it still may work in your case and hopefully we will see you in two to three months".

A second visit never took place.

It was at that time, Muler decided that he wanted to go to Ethiopia to see his family. They are a big family and he is one of nine children. Six of his sisters and brothers still lived in Ethiopia. He has a lot of aunts, uncles and cousins as well. I packed up enough medication and vitamins for three months as instructed and prescribed by the Mexican doctors and he left.

I knew this was so very important for him as it could possibly be the last time he would see his family. All our family and friends encouraged the trip and helped financially as well, as they all thought this would be so good for his morale to see and spend some time with the rest of his family as he hadn't seen them for a few years. They are also a very close knit family.

I stayed behind with Michael and continued to work and try to keep our medical (for the alternative treatment) and other bills at bay. We settled into a somewhat normal routine without Muler, but I was constantly worried. What if he didn't make it home? What if the trip was too much for him? What would I tell our son?

The plan was for him to stay for three months but his health deteriorated rapidly and he started having severe neck, shoulder and lower back pains. These were completely new types of pain that didn't exist before his departure. I insisted he come back home to Toronto immediately. With the support of my bosses at work and friends, I managed to arrange for him to fly back in business class with full support service so he could endure the long flight.

Along with a couple of his close friends, my son and I were waiting for him at the airport and we almost didn't recognize him until he was very close. He had lost so much weight and looked extremely fragile. We were nevertheless very happy to see him and tried our best not to show how shocked we were at the drastic change in his appearance.

Oh, how badly I wished I could go somewhere where nobody could see or hear me, somewhere like the top of a mountain where I could scream my lungs out and let go of all my frustrations and disappointments! That would have helped release the extreme tension that was constantly building up and growing in me, the sad emotion that was piling up, the overall stress that was killing me inside. How much I wished I could let it out!

Is It Ever Going to End?

A month after Muller went to Ethiopia to see his family, I went for a quarterly physical check-up with my doctor which I do frequently due to my being Diabetic and having high cholesterol. During this visit, my doctor noticed a lump on the right side of my thyroid. I never even felt or noticed it before but he took it very seriously and insisted I schedule a biopsy. That news was a terrible blow and I can't begin to tell you how terrified I was!

We had been going through all the stages of treatment with Muler and the outlook was bleak. I couldn't imagine me going through the same thing if this also turned out to be cancer. I wasn't worried about me so much at this point; I was worried sick about my son! What if this is something really bad and my son loses both his mom and dad? The question crept up in my mind. Those of you who have children would probably understand very well what it would feel like if you were in the same situation I was in at that moment.

My biopsy date came and it was over quickly. Now it was a waiting game. Two weeks of waiting seemed like a very, very long time. When the date finally arrived for me to see my doctor who had the results in his hand, it turned out that the biopsy wasn't able to identify if the lump was cancerous or benign. When he checked my neck again, the lumps had multiplied and now there were two additional ones in the right side of my thyroid. He immediately transferred me to one of the best ENT (Ear, Nose and Throat) hospitals in the area for further testing and a decision on whether I needed surgery or not. The surgeon was very well known in Canada and an expert at diagnosing issues such as mine. She knew further tests would not clarify the issue much and that in order to be safe, it would be better to remove half my thyroid. She would then send whatever was removed to the laboratory for in-depth testing and analysis so we would know exactly what we were dealing with.

She advised me that if the results came out benign, everything would be fine but if they were cancerous then she would have me back and remove the rest of my thyroid. I cried and cried. I was just about at the end of my rope both physically and emotionally. What else was I supposed to do? However, the surgeon comforted me that I can live a normal life without my thyroid by taking medication. I was not sure if I wanted to believe her at the time because I felt we were told many things about Muler's cancer that turned out not to be true. I was getting filled with a lot of doubts, negativity and uncertainty - to the extent that my hope was disappearing fast. I was so tired and there were many days I wanted to just give up. The surgery would be scheduled for January and I tried to put it out of my head as Muler and Michael needed me and I had to focus and care for them.

Muler, a week after returning from Ethiopia, was admitted to the Palliative Care at Princess Margaret

Hospital, due to his severe pains. He was taken for further tests and then given pain medications which helped him sleep and rest. I had never seen him as grateful as he was on that first day at the hospital. It was first time in weeks he was able to sleep because the pain had been so tremendous. The test results revealed that his shoulder and lower back pain were caused by huge tumors so they started taking him for radiation every morning to help reduce/shrink the huge lumps. The radiation was somewhat helpful and the lumps shrank. The pain lessened each day, though the heavy doses of pain medication helped a great deal.

The room at the hospital is where he spent the last weeks of his life. He was surrounded by family and friends every day and enjoyed the company. His room was full of flowers and at his request, music played all day, every day. Whenever we were alone even for a minute, he talked to me about his concern as to how I was going to pay all the bills and make the funeral arrangements as he knew well we had no money or means left. By this time, I had cleaned out all our savings including retirement savings and money from the sale of one car (we had two). Up until he talked about the funeral expenses that subject had never even crossed my mind, as I guess I was still in some sort of denial and a little hope still lingered. I was just starting to face the reality that this nightmare would end at some point. Muler would be gone and I would be a single parent raising my son on my own.

I remember January of 2008 and it was very cold. While Muler was in the Palliative Care at the Princess Margaret Hospital, I was finally admitted to Women's College Hospital for my thyroid surgery. Mebrat, one of my best friends, who lived in St. Catherines, a two hour drive from where we lived, took a week off her work to come take care of Michael and help us while we were both at separate hospitals. To this day, I can't thank Mebrat enough. From time to time, she was accompanied by another good friend of ours, Waheeba. My surgery was successful and I was released from hospital in a few days but had to recover at home. While this was great news, there was still the waiting game for the results of the lab tests of the removed lumps.

I insisted that my friends take me to see Muler while I was still in recovery. He was happy to see me and happy that the surgery seemed successful. Reality again kicked in when one of Muler's closest friends, Yemane, took me aside a week into my recovery, and wanted to discuss plans for making funeral arrangement. I stared at him at first and said "are you serious?" He was very understanding and sat me down and talked some sense into me. He knew it was just a matter of time – and a short time at that. He also knew I did not want to face the end. I told him that I didn't have a dime to my name at the moment and I was getting buried deeper in debt by the day.

He immediately cut me off and said, "Don't worry about money, that is what friends and families are for.

Just help us decide the location for service, coffin, and other items."

The next morning, the Palliative Care doctor also took me aside after checking on Muler and told me that he had a maximum of four weeks, if that long, to live and that I needed to start working on a few things. I needed a Will, an Irrevocable Trust, Power of Attorney, and I also needed to start making funeral arrangements. The last thing was that our son Michael, who has just turned eight a couple of weeks earlier had to be told that his dad had cancer and was going to die.

Really?

I asked the doctor in between tears if it was really necessary to tell Michael everything as he was still so young and she insisted, yes, and said that they had professional personnel that could tell him and answer any questions. They set up an appointment for me and my son with the counselor. My gut feeling told me NOT to go about telling my son about the situation in this way, but I obeyed and accepted anyway. I was so tired and could not even bring myself to think about how to approach the subject of Muler's death with my son.

Michael knew his dad was very sick and that he couldn't go to work, or play with him, or take him out anymore but he never knew his dad had cancer. The reason we decided not to tell him was that a year earlier he came home from school crying. When we asked him what happened, he told us that in his class they showed them a video of a famous Canadian youngster namely, Terry Fox, who died of cancer. Muler and I looked at each other and later on agreed that we should never tell him his dad had cancer. I am not sure if that was right or wrong but that's what we decided after seeing him so affected by the movie he watched in school.

The day we went for the appointment for Michael to be informed/told about his dad's real condition is a day that haunts me until present!

Even now, as I write this story, my tears are flowing. The counselor was a female, professional and very soft spoken. She sat us down and told me to try not to interfere in the conversation and as much as possible to sit quietly. It was a boardroom table so I went to a corner and she sat in the other side of the corner facing my son. She chatted with him and asked him how much he knew of his father's illness. He told her his dad was very sick, he used to throw up a lot and that he is at the hospital now.

She asked him if he knew his dad had cancer. That was the shocking moment as he asked, "My dad has cancer?" He actually shouted it.

When she held his hand and confirmed to him he did, Michael cried, for a good 15 minutes and I cried right along with him. She got up and gave each of us a box of tissue. He then, between breathes asked her,

"Can't the doctors at Princess Margaret find cure for him?"

She advised him softly that there is a lot of study going on about treatments but there is no particular cure for cancer at this time yet. He continued to cry. When he wouldn't stop, she then decided to continue to tell him that his dad was going to die in less than a month!

By that time, I got up, hugged my son – I don't recall for how long, we hugged and cried hard, and when she started to speak again, I told her "that is enough, more than enough, we are leaving!" I took my son's hand and left the boardroom and walked out of that hospital. I know that their intention is good but my personal opinion is that this is one of the harshest things to do to a child. He was only eight for heaven's sake. I was extremely upset not just because she had delivered the news so bluntly but also because I had allowed it. Was I overreacting? Well, no matter how much people try to convince me, I still believe it is too harsh to tell a child of that age that his father will die very shortly!

We went back to Muler who was fast asleep. He was sleeping a lot lately. My brother-in-law Berhane was shocked to see us (both Michael and I had swollen eyes) and he stood and arranged a pull-out couch for Michael to lie down on. Michael was so exhausted from crying that he slept for a good four hours afterward.

Gaby Abdelgadir

When he finally woke up, his dad was awake and the room was already full of friends and family.

He ran and hugged his dad and cried. Muler asked him "What happened, Mikey?" Muler cried with him though he had no idea what had happened at the meeting.

Then Michael said to him, "I will find cure for cancer daddy!"

The hospital social worker happened to just pop-in at that time and kicked every visitor out of the room except me. She closed the door so that father and son could have some private time together. She actually sat on the floor and cried as even she, couldn't bear the scene and the pain that my son was enduring. She was a mother of three and couldn't handle what she was watching no more than we could. After all the crying subsided, she went and came back with a lot of gifts for Michael – at least he smiled for the first time and said "thank you". He still has those gifts and I think they are a reminder of the start of his grieving process. He connects them with his father and I would never take that away from him.

I have often wondered about the twists and turns that our path took as we searched for some way to stave off the inevitable end for my husband. When I went into the situation, I was unsure and trusting of what the doctors had to offer. Now I realize that I must advocate for my own health and that of my son.

No one really knows everything about how our bodies work and your intuition is a key element in finding what works for you whether that be through traditional medicine, alternative medicine or a combination of the two. Personally, I wish we had tried alternative medicine much sooner and skipped the chemo altogether. It may not have reversed the eventual outcome, but I believe that Muler would have not suffered near as much and would have had more strength right up until the end. It may have even prolonged his death another year or few months. A lot of people could disagree with me. But then, we all have choices and it is up to each of us to decide what resonates with us most.

As I had said before, everything happens for a reason. Now, as a single parent, I am a strong and active advocate for my own health and my son's. That may not have been the case if things had not transpired as they did. Before Muler's illness I didn't really pay attention to what we ate all that much, but now I do. We eat organic as and when possible, take various vitamins and nutrients and overall I pay much more attention to what my body and intuition is telling me.

We are spiritual beings, but we are not separate from our bodies in this life. We must take care of the vessel we are given even if it is imperfect. Only when both the body and mind are well cared for can we move on into a life of our own design and live our creams.

LESSON # 6

I strongly recommend that people consider natural and alternative medicine whenever possible. We must open ourselves to all the possibilities if we are to achieve a great outcome.

Chapter 7

Chapter 7

A New Approach to Life

If so many of us want to live a fruitful, happy and successful life, then why don't we? I feel that one of the primary factors that cause people to be dissatisfied is that they live their life for others. We can never fulfill another person's perfect idea of who we should be, how we should think or how we should live. To try to do so is an exercise in frustration that leads to unhappiness. To be truly successful, we must find the happiness within ourselves first. Only then can we share that with others.

When I was younger, I lived my life trying to satisfy other people's expectations as many children do. I always did what my Mother wanted – followed her rules, befriended people only after her approval, and even dressed in a way that she liked. I worked hard and I never did anything for myself unless I satisfied the needs of my family first – including my grandmother, uncles, aunts, cousins or anyone else!

In many ways, our family and friends get upset when we don't follow their advice. It is their reality and experiences that they want us to have, not our own. Often they believe they are protecting us from the harsh realities of life, but unfortunately they are also insisting we live from their perspective, even if that perspective is not reality. When we live according to other people's expectations, we have lost the focus of what we really want, why we want it and most importantly, we lose ourselves as to who we are. Other people's happiness will not make us happy. We can't fill a void in our life with someone else's desires. Some people such as our parents or siblings are often determined that we do what they think we should. They think they know what's best for us. Those closest to us, even though their advice is often times well meaning, it can stop us from doing what we actually desire and this contradiction can wreak havoc on our lives. Many people allow others to take control because they are too scared to stand up to them or face life on their own.

This was part of my old self. Now don't get me wrong, it was never that I was weak or anything like that, but I always allowed life to just happen. In particular, I avoided any type of confrontation if I felt it was going to start an argument or a fight. Even though I carried repressed anger around for a lot of my childhood I was also the people pleaser and avoided confrontation with those that mattered to me, like my mother and other family members. I even behaved this way to a certain extent in my life with Muler before his illness. I just wanted everything to be okay and not to rock the boat.

I kept thinking that if everyone else was happy then we would have a happy life, but that is not the case. I had to find my own happiness and the first step to finding that happiness was embracing my own passions and dreams.

Stop Comparing to Others

To be able to live our best life, we need to be able to define what success means to us. Everybody has a different definition of success. Success for us may not necessarily mean the same thing for someone else. For one person, success may mean financial freedom while for another it may mean health and vitality. We can't base our success criteria on what other people have or do not have. Have you ever looked at another individual's success with a twinge of jealousy or envy? What do they know that we are missing? Why them? What gave them the strength to pursue their dreams?

> *The competitor to be feared is one who never bothers about you at all, but goes on making his own business better all the time.*
>
> **– Henry Ford**

We compare ourselves to others when we focus on the lack and limitations in our own lives. Comparison forces us to focus on the abundance and prosperity in someone else's life which reveals a lack in our own lives. When we concentrate too much on what we don't have, we fail to see all that we actually do have. When Muler was so ill, and even to the point of death, I found it very hard to have any gratitude for the life I had. I would walk by people on the street or hear conversations on the train or in stores of people who didn't seem to have a care in the world. They went about life having no idea the depths of despair my life was in. There is no way to compare the two.

It was similar to how I felt shortly after coming to Canada. When I was in Ethiopia and even Sudan, I lived with and around people who shared many of my same experiences. They understood what it was to live through war and how fear changes people. They had done without and pulled themselves together to make it work. There were so many people in Canada who had no idea what that was like. They had grown up in an idyllic life and they had certainly never had to look at a bullet lying on top of their bed that was intended for them! In many ways it is very hard for others to understand how deep those scars are and how much of an effect they can have on a person.

Yet, if we did not have the ability to compare, we couldn't place a value on the things that we desire and I desired that idyllic life. To feel good or feel bad, we have to have something to compare things to. When we compare ourselves to people that are spiritually and physically better than us, it is easy to feel bad. When we compare ourselves to people that haven't attained the spirituality or physical situation that we have, however, it is easier to feel better about ourselves. There will always be those who are better or worse off than us. What I have learned over the years is that nothing about me or my life is good or bad until I compare myself and my life to something or someone else. It is only in making that comparison that causes me to feel less or better than others.

Comparison depends on where we choose to focus our perspective. Are we always looking at those who achieve more and judging ourselves to be not as good - or are we being grateful and thankful for where we are and what we have learned? By making a comparison, we attach a judgment, giving the situation a connotation of being good or bad. In reality, it just "is". We shouldn't consider the lack of what we do not have, but instead be grateful for the abundance that we do have – no matter how small.

Living in the Now

One good question we need to ask ourselves is, "What can really make me happy?" Anything we do in life that can make us fulfilled should be considered a success. Often, when we compare ourselves to others, we only focus on our future wants or past failures. We have to live in the now.

Gaby Abdelgadir

We waste precious time agonizing over past mistakes or worrying about the future. Only by living in the now are we free to focus on what matters right now and give it all our energy. During Muler's illness, I wasted a lot of mental energy worrying about the future or wondering what would have happened if we had chosen the other treatment instead of that one. None of that wondering or worrying made one bit of difference and it wore me down physically and emotionally. You can't have room for healthy relationships if you are wearing yourself down constantly.

I receive daily messages from Neale Donald Walsch from the movie, The Secret, and here is one I would like to share:

It is only this moment that counts.
This moment that matters. Dwelling on
anything else is pointless.
Yesterday is gone, if not forgotten,
and tomorrow is not yet here, so why waste
precious time and mental energy focusing on
either? What is going on right now?
That is the question. And what can you do
right now to make now better?
Make each now better and the future
will take care of itself, while the past
will not matter.

– Neale Donald Walsch

It seems these days that so many of us wait until "the time is just right" to do anything: When the kids are grown. When the right job comes along. When there is enough money. There are a myriad of excuses, but what we do not realize is that the moment we make the decision to do something, the time is **now**. I know for me personally, I put off my dreams time and time again. It seemed there was always someone or something else that I put before myself.

I now have learned that making a decision without knowing the "how" is vital for living in the now. The perfect time for all our goals is right now because there is no perfect time. When the desire for the dream is really strong, that is the time to take action. When an idea is first conceived, that is the time to take action and feed it with your desire. I have had excuses for not working on my dreams and goals for a very long time and that is all they were, excuses.

This was especially true during the years when I was so consumed by taking care of family during the unsettled times in Ethiopia earlier on in my life. Later, after I had a child it seemed there was never enough time to focus on me. Between a full-time job and rushing home to take care of my family's needs, I convinced myself that there was no time to think of anything else. Then came in the diagnosis of Muler's cancer that cancelled any dream or goal I may have been thinking of at the back of my mind.

So many of us don't want to take action because we aren't sure how it would all work out. This was me for a long time. It wasn't until I realized that once I began to take action the "how" would be made known to me. I tried my best to do anything to change our current lifestyle and, most importantly, to keep my son Michael happy after his father's death.

In 2008, a couple of months after Muler passed away, my brother-in-law Dawit, who lived in Washington DC at the time, insisted that we go visit him as that would be a great help for Michael – just to get away and be somewhere outside the usual routine. It was March Break so we did, and Michael and I had a great time for a few days. Family and friends there took us out every day and we went sightseeing and enjoyed the area. It was very helpful just to get us out of the depressing routine we had fallen in to. After our return, Michael had something to talk about for a few weeks other than his dad's death and that was refreshing for us both.

Toward the end of 2008, my long time best friend Hiwet and her husband Mamo who lived in Munich, Germany, begged me to visit, insisting that it would do us both a great deal of good. After sometime and a lot of convincing, I agreed and Michael and I flew to Munich. We left on Boxing Day and spent a wonderful two weeks in Munich including the New Year of 2009.

Although my friends' daughters, Rahel, Martha and Mekdes were a lot older than Michael, they made sure he was well accommodated and entertained. They played games with him, took him out and kept his mind busy. We adults had a lot of catching up to do and Michael had a blast. One of his best memories is visiting the Deutsche Museum and learning something about history. In particular, seeing all the airplanes that had participated in WWII and climbing in to take photos.

Being a typical North American kid, Michael found something else that really got his attention and interested him - eating at the "Most visited McDonald in the World". His eyes were wide open listening to my friend explaining to him that there was a study made which was also in the newspapers that the Munich McDonald was the most visited in the world. I honestly would agree, as this particular McDonald has three floors and I have never ever seen such a long line-up every single day of the week and at any hour of the day! When he got back to Toronto, Michael had something to share with his school friends and would share it with so much excitement.

The two weeks were over soon and we were back home from our lovely vacation - a little rested and refreshed. However, the good feelings never lasted very long with both of us as we would eventually be back to our old pattern of sadness. Michael would start crying missing his dad (on and off) and I continued to have health challenges. Fear, anxiety, worry kept creeping in on me and I had to work hard to keep on fighting them.

It had been almost a year since our last vacation when one day in late 2009, I received an email from Air Miles. While I normally delete any sales emails without reading them, I opened this particular one as something caught my eye. "European Tours – special packages and prices for Air Miles Card Holders". I always loved to travel and I did quite a bit of traveling in my younger and single days. I had promised myself to continue to travel after I retired. Or may be before my retirement? May be my financial situation will somehow improve? Who knows?

I read through the whole email flyer and there was a contact number for detailed information. While finances were still very tight, I decided that another travel could be helpful in breaking the depression that Michael and I were sinking into. So, I called them immediately and got the full information. One of the trips particularly interested me or rather, I thought it would interest Michael. I went with my intuition and made the booking. I thought it would be a lovely surprise birthday gift for Michael as his birthday was coming soon in January. I planned to tell him on Christmas Eve.

The trip had a very organized schedule. The group joining this particular tour would meet up in London, England on a specific date at a specific hotel. Honestly, I had never done any group or package tour in my life before and I was really worried.

God, please make all the people joining us in this two week trip to be very good people, I prayed silently. And God listened to my prayers! We did meet the group on the second day in London and I was so happy and grateful to know that most of the group consisted of older couples, a few were middle aged couples, and then there were two families just like us, i.e. a mother and a son but the sons were all older, There was also a young couple and a couple of single ladies. In short, it was a group of lovely people and the chemistry was instant and amazing. Michael was ten and he was the youngest in the group and quickly became the center of attention. During the entire trip and everywhere we stopped for a break, every one of them was looking out for him! What a blessing!

During our stay in London for two nights and three days, Michael and I, along with some of the families, managed to visit Madame Tussaude, the Buckingham Palace and a lot of other interesting places. Most importantly, Michael had a blast and he was mostly surprised at the way the cars were driven on the left lane (unlike back home in Toronto) and he really liked the London Buses! For me personally, the last I had been in London was back in the nineties and I was kind of shocked at the change in the city. I also had difficulty finding a decent, strong cup of coffee. I love coffee with passion and nothing I tried anywhere seemed to satisfy my addiction.

After the three days, we got in the tour bus and started our journey. We drove to Amsterdam via Belgium and the tour guide told us stories and history of certain places on the way so it was very interesting and entertaining. We would stop every two hours for about 20 minutes, at a certain place where we can use the restrooms, buy food, drinks, snacks and sometimes souvenirs. So while it was very long hours sitting in a bus, the breaks were good for stretching our legs and grabbing a snack, coffee etc.

As soon as we arrived in Amsterdam and we were assigned our hotel rooms, we all went out looking for food and on the way, we stopped by a Cafeteria.

That is when Michael shouted "Mom, this is a very good coffee!"

Surprised, I asked "how do you know that?"

His reply was "that's the same coffee that McDonalds is selling everywhere!"

"Really?" I asked.

My son insisted, "Try it Mom – you will love it, everybody loves McDonald's coffee!"

Hmmm, I think McDonalds should really hire you for advertising for them! I thought.

Up until that moment, I had never purchased coffee at any McDonalds in Toronto or anywhere else. So I bought a small cup just to try it out and guess what? It turned out to be my first decent cup of coffee in almost four days! I hugged Michael and after gulping the small coffee, I bought a large one before we left the Cafeteria. Of course I couldn't eat very well after that and neither could I sleep easily that night. But hey, at least I was happy that I was going to enjoy a good coffee for another day before leaving Amsterdam. My mind was wondering, would Manheim (our next destination in Germany) have a decent coffee? Those of you who are a Starbucks coffee addicts will relate to my concern here.

Some of you may know that Amsterdam's night life is kind of wild and I knew that from my visit in earlier years. So when the tour bus took us for a tour at the core of downtown later in the evening after dinner, I refused to go for a walk with the group as I couldn't take a ten year old to certain types of places to see what the adults were going to see. Everybody else left feeling sorry for me but I assured them not to feel bad as I had seen everything before and I wasn't missing anything. Not only that, but whatever they were going to see wasn't my cup of tea either! The bus driver was with us so we had a nice chat with him. My son however, was bombarding me with questions as to why we were left behind and didn't go with the rest of the group. I had to explain to him that there are certain things that are not good for children to see but he wasn't a happy camper.

The drive from Amsterdam to Germany was absolutely beautiful. I personally enjoyed the scenes of the beautiful and green country sides, the farms and much more. There was always something interesting we were learning from our tour guide and I took notes, lots of notes!

Before we reached Manheim, we stopped in Heidelberg, a city known for its famous Universities. The buildings were very old and very interesting. Not to mention, the churches and the markets. We spent a few hours touring and got in the bus and hit the road again. On our way, we stopped in another beautiful city, Cologne. We had lunch and did a bit of sight-seeing as well as purchased some gift items. We visited a beautiful, very old church and Michael and I went in, prayed and lit candles. We did that in almost every city we stopped at where there was a church nearby. I have no clue what Michael was praying for but I prayed for "health, happiness and serenity". That is all I needed. The more I did that, the more serene I felt. And honestly, I couldn't care less whether it was a church, mosque or Buddhist temple, I would pray anywhere. There is only one God; he is everywhere and he listens!

We finally arrived in Manheim, got settled into our hotels and after showering and changing, we got ready for dinner. This was in a special restaurant, as part of the package and we had a beautiful time, lots of laughter, good food, lots of pictures (thank God for the lovely people in our group, I repeated in my mind and in my heart). We spent two days in Manheim.

We resumed our journey to Switzerland. Luzern, to be specific - also known as "Lucerne". I had been to Geneva, Zurich and a couple of other places in Switzerland but never to Luzern. Our drive there also had a view to die for. We learned a lot about every tiny city or town we passed by. We stopped at a couple of small cities, went on a boat tour where we had lunch and did some gift shopping. We visited a place where they made Swiss Watches and Clocks and they even did a demonstration for us! My son enjoyed that particular demonstration.

I have a cousin, Giuseppe who lives in Neuchatel whom I hadn't seen for over 20 years but we were always in touch by phone. I had told him about our visit to Luzern and gave him the hotel name and an approximate time of our arrival. He took the train for more than two hours and was already waiting for us at the hotel. It was very emotional and we cried! My son got scared and started to cry too not knowing why we were crying. Since I'd last seen my cousin, my mother had passed away, his mother and younger brother had passed and a lot of changes in our lives had taken place. We had to tell Michael that we were okay and it is just that we are meeting after so long. My cousin was shocked and sad staring at me later on while we sat at a McDonalds (to make my son happy). He told me that if I hadn't smiled, he wouldn't have recognized me. This took me off guard.

"Have I changed so much?" I whispered.

"Yes, you lost so much weight. Your beautiful hair is gone and even your color has changed," he replied.

It made me realize that the journey of the past few years, along with my own health issues, had really taken a physical as well as emotional toll on me.

As for him, he looked good despite having health challenges. We also got to do a little catch up on our other cousins who are scattered between Germany, England and Italy. He had to return back to Neuchatel taking the last train, as he had a doctor's appointment the next day so after a few hours, it was time to say goodbye. He gave Michael fifty Euros to buy himself a souvenir and Michael was weeping when he was saying goodbye. Giussepe and I were both surprised to see him weeping.

When I asked him why he was crying he said, "I just meet an uncle for the first time and now I am not going to see him again." This brought us both to tears.

The next day, we went out for a tour in Luzern. While I had seen some other cities and knew that Switzerland is one of the more beautiful countries, Luzern took me completely by surprise. It definitely was beyond my wildest imagination. The mountains, the greenery, the farms, the city itself!

"I could live here forever!" I said to the group and they all laughed and agreed with me.

We spent two nights there. One day was free for everyone to go wherever they want. The second day however was a scheduled tour. Our first stop was going up the mountains. We got into cable cars (also known as Teleferique) four people in each cable car and went up to the highest mountain. I have always had a problem with heights so I closed my eyes all the way as

I got dizzy. Michael and the couple with us, however, were tremendously enjoying the ride. I didn't open my eyes up until we were at a stop. We got off and there was a huge restaurant and a beautiful souvenir shop. The view from the top, where you could see most of the city of Luzern was priceless. The air we breathed was different; very fresh and healthy. After we spent a couple of ours it was time to go back to our next destination. Going down in the cable car however, my son and the others convinced me to try and open my eyes and enjoy the view along the way. I did and it was a great accomplishment for me! An absolutely breathtaking view and I was grateful for being able to see it without getting the usual dizziness.

Our second destination was a visit to a farm. When we arrived there, there were horse carts waiting for us to take us for a tour. Michael was ecstatic as this was a very new and exciting experience for him. While I was thoroughly enjoying the ride and the stories about the traditions and living style of the farmers told by the guide, I was happier to see my son so excited and beaming all the way! Along the way of trying to make my son happy, I had the time of my life. After we were done with the tour, we were stopped at the house of one of the horse cart riders. We were greeted by his wife who spoke very little English but was extremely pleasant and welcoming. To our group's surprise, there was lunch ready for us. All organic! Organic meat, organic cheese, organic milk and even their juices were organic.

While eating, I looked at my group and said to them "if I ever win a $50 million lottery or more, the first thing I would do is fly here and buy a property!" They all laughed and most agreed with me that they would definitely do the same.

The three days of paradise were over and we left on the way to our last destination, Paris, France. The ride from Luzern to Paris was yet another memorable one. We saw and learned a lot of history along the way. We saw beautiful small towns, smaller cities, farms and all in all, amazing view.

We arrived in Paris by early afternoon and after we checked in our hotel rooms, there was already a pre-planned arrangement for us to go on a boat tour of part of Paris in the evening with a few stops along the way. A stop to the Eiffel Tower was one of them. Since it was dark by then, the tower was lit up beautifully! When some of the groups were ready to go up the tower and I asked Michael if he wants to join the families, he said no.

Personally, I had been in Paris three times before and I never went up the Eiffel Tower due to my problems with height and getting dizzy. So I wasn't going to do so now.

But when I asked Michael why he wouldn't go with the families, his reply was "CN Tower is a lot higher that the Eiffel Tower so I really don't have to go up there".

Sigh... CN Tower (The Canadian National Tower) at the time of our travel was the highest free-standing tower in the world so he was right about that. But I tried to explain to him that from CN Tower he could see the city of Toronto but from the Eiffel Tower he would have a good view of the city of Paris therefore, it is a different experience.

He wouldn't and I thought to myself, it's my fault; he would have gone if I did – may be another time when he is older and doesn't need me.

The next day in Paris was also very well organized by the tour guide. We took off to Versailles and visited all the beautiful places that this amazing city offers. We visited the Chateau de Versailles Gardens; The Art Gallery, Hall of Mirrors and everything the Palace had to offer. We spent a good five to six hours as there was just so much to see, to read, to learn and to absorb. By the afternoon, we returned back to our hotels to rest and got ready for the evening event.

The evening event however, was not for me and Michael. The arrangement that was made for the group was to go for a dinner and a show at "Lido". Lido is one of the very well-known and very entertaining Cabarets (or night club) located in the heart of Champs-Elysees. This was definitely not a place for a ten year old to visit. Thank goodness I had seen it years ago in my single days. Everybody felt so sad for me and Michael again but I assured them that we would go for long walks along the beautiful Champs-Elysees, have a nice dinner somewhere and have a mother and son time and that they should just go and have fun. I was excited for them as this was the first time they would visit Lido (and for most of them visiting Europe in general). So while the rest of the group went for the show, Michael and I enjoyed a long walk and sightseeing, had a nice dinner followed by an ice-cream for him and a nice coffee for myself (yes, they have a nice coffee) and eventually went back to our hotel.

The next day was our last day of the trip. It was a free day for everyone to do whatever so half of us agreed to go to The Louvre Museum while the other half wanted to go downtown shopping. For me it wasn't my first time to visit The Louvre either but I wanted Michael to see it and learn about the history of France and all of its earlier leaders. We spent most of the day there and Michael thoroughly enjoyed it.

As a group, we had our last dinner together and lots of email and phone numbers were exchanged. It actually was a bit emotional to say good-bye. When we went to the hotel, we all hugged, some wept and the most amazing thing that happened to me was some of the older travelers pulled me aside to say, "you have raised such a good child, we have never seen a 10 year old so well behaved." That took me off guard and I joined in the crying. Yes, I am proud of the way I am raising my son. He is a very good kid – God Bless him.

It was really great to return home. This trip was something we needed, especially for Michael. He couldn't stop talking about his experiences for quite a long while! It was really essential that we took a break from all our worries and just experience life and all the beauty it offers.

This is a difficult concept for some to enjoy the process of living each day. But now, I strive daily to live in the now. Like most people, I struggle with old habitual ways of thinking and acting that keep me from stepping out and living in the now as I know I should. The old habitual patterns of thinking are comfortable in some ways as they keep me from taking risks.

Unfortunately, far too many of us ever live our lives to our fullest potential because we aren't willing to step out of that comfort zone. We get cozy in life with our daily and weekly routines, and can almost set our clock by what events happen throughout the week. The greatest difficulty that we have is overcoming fear, letting go of old hurts and unrealistic expectations and forming new habits. Living in the now brings me up against uncomfortable feelings as my paradigms fight to keep things the same instead of experiencing the new and different. We live in a world where many people allow themselves to be limited by their fears, unrealistic expectations and comparison to others. Many times we have to release our fears before we can move to freedom.

Gaby Abdelgadir

Self-Growth

We were created to constantly expand, evolve and grow, and if we don't, then each day that passes puts our goals and dreams that much further away. Whether we realize it or not being creative is part of our nature. We are all created as beings of growth. We are beings in a constant state of motion. When we feel unhappy or have some vague feeling that something is wrong, it is because we are not focused on moving forward. Our inner creative self is always striving for expansion and growth. Our natural desire is to create something new; something that has never been created before. The power within gives us focus for our creative desires. When we move through life with this gift but not acting on it, we are resisting our inner creative nature. It is that resistance to our very nature that creates anxiety and tension in our lives.

The movie The Secret introduced me to Bob Proctor and many others in the field of personal development. Studying with Bob has helped me turn my life around. From the anger and frustration I was carrying around on my shoulders, to someone who now strongly believes in "Letting go and Letting God". It has transformed the way I think and the way I live my life now.

I have gone from believing that I was obligated to put up with negative people (whether they were family, friends or colleagues) to gradually letting go of all the people who didn't serve me or my health in any way, while still wishing them all the best in their lives. This practice was very hard but I made it happen. I changed the list of people I connect with in my daily life, thus changing my life to a more positive experience.

While I was always into self-development and did a few courses from Anthony Robbins, Dr. Joe Vitale, and others, it wasn't until I became a dedicated student of Bob Proctor that I made the actual change. I met coaches and mentors like Dr. Gay Hendricks, Mary Morrissey, Peggy McColl, Sandy Gallagher and many, many more. I have met so many wonderful people who share the same beliefs, principles and interests as I do. And I have made a few very good friends along the way.

Still, I have had some doubts about what I could do in the future. In particular, since becoming a single mother and continuing to experience various health issues. Bob not only helped me believe in myself again, but he taught me the steps of having a family/life balance. I used to think that it has to be all or nothing. But it doesn't. You can have it all in life, you just have to balance the things you want.

I am now deep into spirituality and self-development. At home, I listen to personal development audio lessons repeatedly. Since I do a lot of driving, in my car I have the CDs of Napoleon Hill, Earl Nightingale, Bob Proctor. I also have the teachings of Abraham by Ester and Jerry Hicks, Christie Marie

Sheldon, James Allen and many, many more that I listen to.

For the last year and a half, my health has improved tremendously to the extent that I was never sick once over a continuous 12 months. I learned to try and avoid watching the news, which is filled with so much negativity, and therefore I no longer feel fear when they report on all the shootings, stabbings and fighting around the world. If there is anything important I need to know, one of my friends will tell me. I now only watch comedy or something inspirational such as Oprah's Life Classes, Joel Osteen's Sunday teachings and a few others. I record all the ones that resonate with me to watch over and over again.

I no longer have the attitude of, "you will have to pay for hurting me". I now approach problems with, "I forgive you and I am letting you go".

Previously, in particular during my younger days, I always wanted more and was never satisfied. I recall my Mom telling me, "take the stairs one-step-at a time because if you try to take four steps at a time, you could fall and break part of your body". She was right and that lesson transcends all parts of my life.

Now, I am satisfied with the smallest things that I have. I am always grateful for each new day instead of constantly striving for a 'better' day. I now notice and appreciate the little things in life that I used to take for granted. As a matter of fact, I now own a Gratitude

Journal where I write my daily gratitude every morning. It boosts my energy for the day. Not only that, I am teaching my son to count at least five things he is grateful for each day and to say "thank you" before he says his prayer at bed time.

The Importance of a Good Mastermind Group

I have to say that I have a great Mastermind Group. For those unfamiliar, a mastermind group is a group of like-minded people who meet to support one another's goals and dreams. Not only are these groups supremely creative, they also give each member accountability for the steps they are taking to meet those goals.

Not surprisingly, the group I am in are all from different backgrounds and yet we all share the same values and interests. We are a group of men and women from Australia, USA, Chile and Canada. We are all students of Bob Proctor and we were assigned to this Mastermind Group while attending a thirteen month Bob Proctor Coaching Program.

Even though we have already completed the Coaching Program, we were given the opportunity to continue our Masterminding which we have done as it is so beneficial. We are on a weekly one hour call where we first briefly discuss our wins of the week followed by any challenges that any one of us may have had. We all give and receive needed advice or help. We spend between 15-20 minutes discussing some of our assigned studies - be it from a certain book we are reading or revisit some of the things we learned and remind one another of what we learned, where we needed improvement and so forth.

In between our weekly calls, we also exchange emails with ideas for MSI's (multiple sources of income) or any new program that would be beneficial to all of us, for example, a new book that is a "must read". I found that having accountability partners like my own amazing Mastermind Group, who are very serious in following up with your weekly goals, keeping you accountable and pushing you go forward, has helped me a lot in keeping my goals on track.

Like every other person, I sometimes feel that time is flying by much faster than I would like and I don't have a lot of time to complete some of my "to-do" list. But as soon as I think of my upcoming weekly Mastermind call and the fact that I have to report what I have accomplished, I immediately re-write my to do list and make sure I have completed my weekly goals before our call.

I honestly feel that had I not been part of this amazing group and experienced how serious everyone is about improving their life and reaching their specific goals, I probably wouldn't be writing this book right now!

It is an understanding that the desires of my heart have been made known to God and that they are happening now. The awareness might not all be there yet, but once the idea has been born and combined with desire and focus, it is created. When we stop comparing ourselves to others, live in the now, and grow personally and spiritually, we are not ruled by our conscious mind. Rather, we are choosing our thoughts and creating instead of reacting to situations. We are able to change the results in our lives and create things to the order that we desire. We can form new bigger and better results.

LESSON # 7

Stop living in the past or future. Take time to breathe and live in the now developing healthy relationships with both yourself and those around you.

Chapter 8

Chapter 8

Gratitude

When it comes to friends and family, we have always been blessed. While I don't personally have family members here in Canada, I am blessed and consider myself one of the luckiest human beings when it comes to friends. Muler not only had wonderful friends but he had a huge family circle. Every weekend, our home was full of family and friends. There was no time to think about the problems or worries with so many faces and so much joy around. He really looked forward to the weekends when he was surrounded by all his friends and family and it helped him forget about his pain, even if it was temporary. All of them knew we needed their positive energy and they gladly shared!

One definition of gratitude is "the state of being grateful." What does it mean to be thankful and why is it so important? Over the course of our life, we get so conditioned to say a quick "thank you" that we lose touch with what it means to really **feel** gratitude.

Gratitude is one of the most powerful and healing emotions we can express as humans. Why is gratitude such a powerful emotion? In a true state of gratitude, we tap into the source where all blessings come from. When we truly feel grateful for something, we are in a state of love and peace which allows us to find more joy, feel more inspired and tap into our creativity. In a state of gratitude, life flows easily and struggles that once seemed insurmountable now become tiny inconveniences.

When you change the way you look at things,
the things you look at, change.

– Dr. Wayne Dyer

One of the most powerful tools we can utilize in seeing something from another point of view is gratitude. When looking for a different way to view a situation, we need to ask ourselves "what we can be grateful for?" Nothing is good or bad until we compare it to something else, so we must step back and form a new perspective of the events in our lives. Every event has both a negative and positive aspect and once we see that even in the darkest circumstances how an event changed us, and helped us grow, then we can embrace that positive energy of gratitude.

I know this seems counterintuitive. How are we supposed to be thankful for something that can potentially cause us physical or mental anguish? How can something that is bad possibly be good for us? The experiences in our lives that can be quite uncomfortable (or downright miserable) can also be the most powerful experiences we can have to help us learn and grow by quantum leaps and bounds. Once we learn to master the concept of failure as a learning tool, we are empowered to take charge of our own perception and take the necessary steps to correct our course in this life.

Once we are able to view any trials and tribulations through the lens of gratitude, the problems seem small and easy to overcome. Gratitude shelters us from the storms of life by giving us a sense of peace and happiness. For every bad there is a good, and when we experience the unpleasant, we are able to enjoy the pleasant at a deeper level than before.

About a year or so after returning home (to Asmara from our stay in Tigray during the war), one morning my Mom surprised me by telling me that she was going to travel to the cities where we spent nights while travelling, both ways. She had made arrangement for a couple of our neighbours to sleep in our house so that I was not alone.

When I asked her why she had to go, her answer was, "Think about those people who helped me get home and the people who help us when we were travelling to Tigray. They were poor, yet they insisted their children sleep on the floor to allow us to sleep on a bed. They didn't have much, yet they cooked a very nice dinner for us followed by a nice breakfast the next morning before our departure. I am going to visit each one of them to say thank you for everything you have done for us and let them know that we will never forget them - ever."

She said she would be back in two days. She did go back; this time in buses and convoys and she actually was able to carry a luggage full of gifts for her visit. Upon her return, she said that they all cried when they saw her. They were so grateful that she made a special trip just to see them. What a beautiful lesson it was for me to never forget the importance of showing gratitude.

A deep feeling of gratitude for all the good and bad we have in our life opens the Universe's doors for abundance to flow to us. We can't fall into the thought process that gratitude comes only after we have received the good. Instead, we have to be grateful for all things, past and present. We must be willing and able to receive, and gratitude enables us to accept the gifts from the Universe.

During all those tough years of Muler's illness followed by my own health scares, I happened to work for one of the best corporate companies in the world. A firm that strongly believes and advocates family life balance and is very big on diversity. I don't know of many people who can say that about their workplaces (even today as I no longer work there). After all we had been through, and knowing the fact that I had to be with Muler at the hospital a couple of times a week, the day came when I had to tell my boss, Danny Cisterna, a Partner at Deloitte.

Danny is one of the sweetest, most compassionate and helpful human beings I have ever come across. The whole team I worked with were unbelievably supportive. They truly cared and made sure to remind me that they were all there for me if I needed help in any way or at any time! How lucky can someone be? Danny was extremely shocked when I told him the story and I sat there in his office and cried for what it seemed a good ten minutes. He handed me a box of tissue and told me to let it out and not hold back – and I didn't. He told me that he would make some calls and that I shouldn't worry about my once or sometimes twice a week absences.

Danny did make his calls and everyone in the firm from top management leaders, namely, Andrew Dunn, to Human Resources; to the whole group at the Indirect Tax team, to all the EAs. All of them were extremely supportive and it was beyond my expectation. Even now, I don't know how I would have survived the following few years, had I not been given all the support and work flexibility. In particular, because I was the only bread winner during Muler's illness. It is a stark illustration that even at the depths of despair we can find gratitude for those that help us along the way.

My Gratitude

As I said earlier on, I consider myself one of the most blessed and lucky people on earth. Especially, when it comes to friends. I don't have sisters but God has granted me with something bigger and better. Very good, sincere, honest, helpful and extremely loyal friends that always are there for me, who would defend me in my absence and most importantly, who believe in me and love me for who I am. It is something that all the money in the world cannot buy. It is a priceless gift. Not too many people can say that about their friends. I see so many people gossip about their so called friends or get jealous of what others have, but not me. Having this blessing is something that I will never, ever take for granted.

> *Acknowledging the good that you already have in your life is the foundation for all abundance.*
>
> **– Eckhart Tolle**

In so many ways, I am also very grateful for all the hardships I had to go through in my life. You know why? Because they made me a very strong woman. While I was always considered a kind and compassionate person by nature, all the ups and downs of life have thought me to become even more compassionate, but also resilient. I am now more understanding, a better listener and even more helpful to people than I was before tragedy struck my family. I now give more focus to people who are undergoing some kind of hardship, be it due to health, relationships or anything else. I make it my job to be there for them and help raise their vibration. Moral support is something priceless and as people were there for me once, now I strive to be there for others. Help and support is not always about giving away money. People need someone to listen to them when they need an ear and offer a shoulder when they need to have a good cry.

I am very grateful for the good times that I had in between hardships. I am grateful that I was able to fulfill some of my dreams. Travelling the world was one of those dreams I always had and I am grateful to have travelled some. I had the privilege to visit some European countries. I have seen almost all the big cities in Germany several times. I have visited England, Switzerland, Holland, Spain, and Tenerife Island. I have visited Italy, France and even Yugoslavia (before the war and is now divided into God knows how many countries). I have had the chance to visit Hong Kong in China. And of course, I lived in two different African countries, namely, Sudan and Ethiopia. I also visited Egypt several times. I had the opportunity to live and work in the Middle East (UAE) – the last place I lived before I immigrated to Canada. All of these experiences taught me so much about people and though it is easy to think that we are all very different, my travels taught me that deep down, we are all really the same.

I am grateful for my decision to immigrate to Canada, a country that I call home now. A country so beautiful and well diversified and friendly that there is no other place I would rather be. A country where everyone has a voice and respect. A place where I can be myself and not be judged just because I am a woman. Yes, I am now (and have been for the last 15 years) a proud Canadian Citizen.

Having said that, I will always cherish my background, my parents' background and all my history. Since my arrival in Toronto in January 1997, life in general has been great. It wasn't difficult for me to get a good job quickly due to my extensive experience in my field.

While there was absolutely no plan or agenda for me to meet anyone and that my decision was to continue my travel around the world, I met Muler at a friend's house. I believe this was meant to be and to this day, I believe that it was my destiny to meet him and to have my amazing son, Michael.

I am grateful knowing that if any one of my friends needs me anywhere and I am able to, I can now be of assistance to them as they have been to me all these years.

I am also extremely grateful for what I have learned from my Mom. In spite of my difficult upbringing and the dominating personality that my mom may have had, she was one of the most independent, strong, wise and smart women I have ever, or probably will ever, know. The life lessons I learned from her have definitely helped me along the way and continue to this day.

Last but not least, I am in deep gratitude to God the Almighty for blessing me with my son Michael. Not only is he well mannered, loving, caring, respectful towards others and very compassionate, in my eyes he is the most handsome, smart and funny child a mother could ever be blessed with!

LESSON #8

Be grateful even for the smallest support you get from family, friends and colleagues! Gratitude brings more of what you are grateful for – that is for sure!

Chapter 9

Chapter 9

The Big Picture

As you have read throughout these pages, I have gone through a lot of challenges in my life, some big and some small. I am proud to say that I have overcome all of them and I have learned a lot along the way - not only about how to handle such things, but about myself as a person.

However, it does not mean that challenges cease at any point in time. I have learned that we will always be faced with life's obstacles from time to time but now I have gained the tools to handle them in a positive way, no matter the situation.

I have learned how important it is to accept whatever comes our way with Grace and then take a deep breath and leave it alone for a little while. There are things we can't control in this life but we can control our reaction to them and how we allow the circumstance to affect our lives.

One of the greatest lessons I have learned is to take your time before you make any sort of decision or take any action. Anything done in haste most of the time turns out to be either ill advised or a big mistake. By calming your mind and allowing your intuition to guide you, your decisions will bring you a step closer to that ultimate happiness you seek.

Meditation is one thing that I have started in the last two years that has helped me stay calm and that has interjected a lot of peace in my life. This in turn helps me make the right decisions when I am unexpectedly faced with something unforeseen. I encourage you to seek out and try new things and then adopt those that help you achieve your own life balance that is so important.

I have also learned that the more you complain, the more you attract things to complain about. I understand now how important it is to shut out as much negativity as possible from my daily life and continue to strive to lead a very positive existing. This allows me to focus on the now and choose positive uplifting thoughts during my day.

Up until a few years ago, I got upset at each new challenge or hardship I faced. I used to say, "Is this ever going to end? When on earth am I going to have a break in life? Why are these things happing to me?"

But I have now learned that this sort of attitude only brought more hurt into my life. The more upset I got, the worse things became and my own health suffered.

Instead of questioning, "why are these things happening to me?" I now ask, "okay, now what is the best way to handle this?" And then allow some time to pass before I make a decision.

When you accept whatever challenge you face, instead of complaining, trust that it will be solved somehow; instead of doubting, stay calm and focus on the good that may come out of this; instead of getting upset or angry, **believe** that a solution or an idea will come to you – and it will, guaranteed.

I don't know if this book will help you. I sure hope it does, but please understand that it is not the only reason why I wrote it. I wrote this book because I have so much joy for all these experiences that I wanted to share a record of the lessons I have learned from them. Hopefully, they will offer peace and courage to those who are also going through trying circumstances.

One day, when my son is much older, perhaps even after I am gone, he will read these words and understand how much he was loved. I want him to know that it is never too late to have the life he desires – any type of life – and that it is up to him to choose. If I never accomplish one more thing in my life, this is enough. To share my love and hope for a wonderful, beautiful tomorrow.

I would like to conclude my book by sharing my favourite Irish blessing to you:

May the road rise up to meet you,

May the wind be always at your back,

May the sun shine warm upon your fields,

And May God hold you in the hollow of His Hand.

Amen!

Acknowledgements

I would like to take a moment to thank all the people who have helped me and my family during the tough years between 2005 – 2008.

At Deloitte:

All Management Consulting and Human Resources Team

To all the amazing Senior Administrative Assistants

To all the Indirect Tax Team without exception – thank you for your unbelievable support.

Special gratitude to:

Danny Cisterna, Partner (and his amazing wife Joan Devine)

Sandra Slaats, Partner

Gaby Abdelgadir

Mary Esteves, Associate Partner

Jason Riche, Partner (now at Calgary office)

Rory Pike, Partner

Angela Grant, Associate Partner

Glynis Henry, Partner

Doug Myrden, Partner

To those whose support I so much appreciated who have left Deloitte since:

Andrew W. Dunn, Managing Partner and COO, Altas Partners LP

Bob Sacco, Principal, CanTradeGlobal

Rick Parker, Partner (retired)

Jim Vincze, Partner (retired)

Sid Paquette, Omers

To Muler's friends who were always by his side and brought a smile to his face:

Asmelash Berhane

Fetsum Gebremichael & Family

Asefa Mengesha & Family

Woldemariam Bahta & Family

Yemane Gebregziabher & Family

Yemane Asefa & Family

Kidane Woldemariam & Family

Abebe & Azeb - Edmonton

Yalem Meresa and Family

Askalu Atsbaha and your amazing siblings Dawit, Berhane and Letish – Washington

Yerusalem (Kiki) - Washington

To my amazing brothers-in-law:

Berhane Fessaha and Dawit Fessaha

To all Muler's cousins

Special gratitude to Dina Mesfin – Danduni, you may be Muler's cousin but you are the sister that my Mom never gave me. Thank you for always being there for me and for inspiring me! That goes for you too, Fasil.

To the one and only Berhe Family:

Elsa, Genet, Hiwet, Abeba, Bisrat and of course Awetash Abraha, Menbere Biadgo - I want to add that you are the family that God gave me although through Muler. Thank you for always being there for me and treating me like one of your sister!

Gaby Abdelgadir

I also would like to thank all the Ethiopian community and the congregation of St. Michael's Orthodox Church for all their support.

To all doctors, nurses and staff at the Princess Margaret Hospital and in particular the Palliative Care.

To my lifetime friends who have been more than sisters:

Thea Cosma - Toronto

Mebrat Males – Toronto

Waheeba Elrefaine, Toronto

Nagwa Fakhoury - Toronto

Diana Brown – Abu Dhabi

Nina Katbeh – Abu Dhabi

Haifa Shafati – Abu Dhabi

Manal Abdulhamid – Abu Dhabi

Kerbanu Mehta – Abu Dhabi

Hiwet Haile & Family – Munich

Aster Berhane – Khartoum

Angela Barham, Toronto

To my amazing Mastermind Group:

Larry Hummond, Tim Ainsworth, Sybella Sheppard, Grant Richardson and Jess Brito – thank you for your support during my writing journey.

Thanks to Dee Burks, my publisher for her amazing guidance and support.

About the Author

Gaby Abdelgadir has a Business Administration Diploma with over 30 years of international experience working with corporate companies as a Legal Assistant, Executive and Senior Administrative Assistant. Gaby has a deep passion for continuous self-development and spirituality. Gaby is an avid reader and loves travel, art, writing and spending quality time with family and friends.